6+

MLA – 123+ (Wks. cit.
APA – 143+ (Ref.s)
ACS – 145+ (Ref.s)

218-30 – srces

Four Other Systems You Might Need

FINDING ANSWERS
A Guide to Conducting and Reporting Research

Elaine Hughes
Jay Silverman
Diana Roberts Wienbroer

Nassau Community College
Garden City, New York

HarperCollinsCollegePublishers

Acquisitions Editor: Patricia Rossi
Project Coordination and Text Design: Proof Positive/Farrowlyne Associates, Inc.
Cover Design: Kay Petronio
Production Manager: Kewal Sharma
Compositor: Proof Positive/Farrowlyne Associates, Inc.
Printer and Binder: R.R. Donnelley & Sons Company
Cover Printer: The Lehigh Press, Inc.

Credits:
On pp. 40–42 © 1993 Carlyle Systems Inc., Carlyle Systems online catalog; and
on p. 42 © 1993 Information Access Company, Magazine Index™

Finding Answers: A Guide to Conducting and Reporting Research, First Edition
Copyright © 1994 by Elaine Hughes, Jay Silverman, and Diana Roberts Wienbroer

Library of Congress Cataloging-in-Publication Data

Hughes, Elaine.
    Finding answers: a guide to conducting and reporting research/
Elaine Hughes, Jay Silverman, Diana Roberts Wienbroer.
        p.   cm.
    Includes bibliographical references (p.) and index.
    ISBN 0-06-501408-1
    1. Report Writing—Handbooks, manuals, etc.   2. Research—
Handbooks, manuals, etc.   I. Silverman, Jay, 1947–
II. Wienbroer, Diana Roberts.   III. Title.
LB2369.H835   1993
808'.02—dc20

                                                      93-21888
                                                          CIP

93 94 95 96 9 8 7 6 5 4 3 2 1

Table of Contents

Part IV   Giving Credit to Your Sources: 107
Documentation

(See the inside back cover for a listing of documentation
   formats.)

Preface

The purpose of *Finding Answers: A Guide to Conducting and Reporting Research* is to build a bridge between traditional academic research—the kind you do for a term paper—and life-long research—the kind you do when you choose a profession. We believe that the skills you learn by doing academic research will make you a more effective communicator and will be useful to you long after college. We also believe that you can find interesting angles for college research by drawing on your personal interests and passions.

Research in college comes in different shapes and sizes. Usually it means preparing a single term paper. This book guides you through every step in writing one, from finding a topic you can care about, through the research, all the way to the final, polished manuscript. But we also cover more specialized projects, such as literature papers, science reports, interviews, and family histories. And we give suggestions for how to proceed through an extended project such as a series of papers on one topic or an independent study project.

After college, you may conduct research as part of your career (marketing, journalism, product development, and so forth), and you certainly will conduct research in your private life. At every stage of life, you will find yourself in need of information in order to make wise choices for yourself and your family. We believe that you can become a more powerful and successful person if you can connect the skills of a researcher to your needs and passions in life. Throughout this book we will be helping you—both through conventional and unconventional means—to succeed in any research project, both in college and beyond.

Acknowledgments

Heartfelt thanks go to our most careful and patient readers: Nell Ann Pickett, Hinds Community College; Lynn Miller, Proof Positive/Farrowlyne Associates, Inc.; and Beverly Jensen.

Finding Answers also was thoughtfully reviewed by Chris Anderson, Oregon State University; Steve Berman, Oakland Community College; Lynda Corbin, San Diego Mesa College; Jan Geesaman, College of DuPage; Casey Gilson, Broward Community College; Stephen Hahn, William Paterson College; Phyllis Luck, Broward Community College; Polly Marshall, Hinds Community College; Robert McCoy, Kent State University; and Dan McLeod, San Diego State University.

Lance Silverman gave us valuable ideas for the chapter on scientific research. Vera Jerwick, Marilyn Rosenthal, and other members of the library staff at Nassau Community College made many suggestions for the chapters on the library. Kirtley Wienbroer and Michael Roughsedge gave us insights from students' perspectives.

The students in our composition and literature classes at Nassau Community College have worked with various drafts of *Finding Answers;* their responses have shaped many of our decisions about the book. In addition, a number of students have contributed essays, parts of essays, and specific research topics; these students include Eric Jergenson, Chris McDonnell, Steven Pangiotidis, Donna Pesiri, Fran Silverman, Thomas Sperandeo, and Barney Yee.

Finally, we wish to thank our editors at HarperCollins, Patricia Rossi and Mark Scott, for their knowledge, their enthusiasm, and their graciousness. We have always felt their support. At every turn, they have done whatever it took to answer our questions and to realize our ideas.

Part One

Starting Where You Are Right Now

Chapter

1

Research Gives You Power

Research gives you power—the power to get what you want. Research can help you to choose a college, check out a company you might work for, buy a house, or learn your legal rights. Sometimes research means simply finding the right person to consult, asking first one person who then leads you to another who leads you to another and so on. More often you will need to go further and read newspaper or magazine articles, public documents, books, or manuals. Taking the time to do even a little research can give you the edge in most situations. In fact, the ability to conduct solid research can affect your entire life—and can even save your life.

Think, for example, of how people react when they have a serious injury or illness. So often they become passive and merely react to their symptoms and put themselves into a doctor's hands without asking questions about the treatment. But if you have the habits and the skills of research, you can take a much more active role in your recovery. You can learn about your condition—what to expect and how to cope. You can get second and third opinions, and so perhaps discover a more appropriate treatment. You can find support groups or specialized therapists. In short, you can approach your problem in an informed way and know the important questions to ask. The results could make a crucial difference in how fully and quickly you recover.

Finding a Home in Any Research Assignment

Even though research in your personal life can give you power, writing research papers in college can make many students feel powerless. They see research papers as an obstacle course they have to get through. The process seems overwhelming.

To gain power over your research project, you need to establish a feeling of authority. This means finding your own personal angle on the topic or finding the aspect of the topic that you care about. If you can *find a home* in your topic, then you can *feel at home* writing a research paper.

Often you'll be free to choose a topic for research. As much as possible, you should choose a topic that you feel passionate about—something that heats up your blood and makes you want to find out everything you can about it. Don't settle for anything you feel indifferent about. If you choose a topic that really matters to you, you will be doing yourself a favor. Not only will you have the momentum to do the research, but you will have an opportunity to learn information that you really want to know.

When You Face a "Boring" Topic

Of course, many times you will find yourself with an assigned topic. If you're lucky, you will have a natural interest in the subject, but sometimes the subject will mean nothing to you. Even in the most boring topic, however, you can find some corner that has meaning for you. Take the time necessary to discover an aspect that truly interests you. The trick to doing well (and perhaps even enjoying the process) is to search for what is real to you in the subject. Don't dismiss any subject as a waste of time.

Suppose you are given the remote topic of "The Gods of Mesopotamia." Here is a religion that no one has believed in for two thousand years. What in this subject can matter to you? You can start to give life to this topic by writing down questions that occur to you. Start with the most obvious questions and let these lead to more complex ones:

Who were the Mesopotamians?

When and where did they live?

Who were their gods?

Were they nature gods—sun, moon?

What were other religions of the time?

Did Mesopotamian religion contribute to our religions?

Perhaps you feel that religion is less important than other aspects of life—such as economics or love. You may be able to think of questions that connect the assigned topic to your real interests: Does the religion of the Mesopotamians fit in with the way they organized their economy or personal relationships? You might end up with a topic such as the link between agriculture and Mesopotamian religion or the relationship between Mesopotamian marriages and religious myths.

The connection between academic research and the personal research that you will conduct all through life lies in asking questions that matter to you. In your personal and professional life, the questions will be pressing:

How do I find a job that I like?

How do I choose the right school—for myself or for my children?

Where do I want to live?

How do I make my business succeed?

How do I stay healthy?

The same sense of urgency can make academic research meaningful. In academic research, you should look for intriguing, even pressing, questions and set about answering them with determination. You will be building a habit of mind and a set of skills that will make you a true researcher—for life.

Chapter 2

Finding a Topic You Care About

To discover a topic that matters to you, you need to start where you are right now and build on your life-long interests and natural preferences. Taking time to connect your assignment to your personal interests is not a waste of time: It will motivate you to dig into research and provide a clear direction in which to move.

This chapter takes you through four crucial steps in finding a topic you care about: *Brainstorming, freewriting, formulating questions,* and *defining goals.* In order to begin, all you need is a notebook and a pen. Set aside some quiet time away from distractions.

If you work through this chapter carefully, you will end up with a specific topic and will know exactly what you want to learn about it.

Brainstorming

Your brain contains a vast amount of information that you aren't usually conscious of until you have to use it. All this information is a tremendous resource; but in order to get the benefits of this resource, you must spend some time coaxing your brain—which you can do through *brainstorming.*

Brainstorming is a process of focusing on one subject for a period of time in order to obtain a cluster of bright ideas.

Brainstorming means:

- Making many lists rapidly
- Sticking with the subject and going over it several times

- Pushing your brain until you feel you have exhausted every possibility
- Making diagrams, sketches, or clusters of ideas

A Waste of Time?

Brainstorming needs unhurried time. Yet most students are in a hurry and want to get to the library, line up some sources, and start writing. To them, brainstorming sounds like delay and unnecessary work. In fact, the opposite is true: Taking time now to brainstorm will save you much more time later because you will proceed with a clear sense of the project. You will go to the library with specific questions and ideas in mind.

Creation Begins with Chaos

Brainstorming is by its nature chaotic, so it may seem uncomfortable to you at first. At this stage, do not try to be organized. When you're really in the flow of brainstorming, more ideas will come to you than you can comfortably manage. But don't let the onslaught of ideas that seem to come from nowhere overwhelm you. If you keep pushing through, you'll be rewarded with better ideas than you could have discovered through a totally controlled approach.

The following pages show you how to brainstorm when you have an assigned topic *or* when you have an open topic.

When You Have Been Assigned a General Topic

When you've been assigned general topic guidelines, here is a method for finding a specific topic you can study with enthusiasm. Let's say you are taking a course in American literature since 1865, and you've been asked to write a research paper on a topic related to the course. Put "American Literature" at the top of the page.

Now make a list of every subtopic you can think of. Your list could include the following:

development of the short story

immigrant literature

African-American literature

Death of A Salesman

Stephen Crane

Willa Cather's stories

naturalism

social protest

the Jazz Age

Go back and circle three or four of the words or ideas which seem most important to you. Suppose you circle "immigrant literature" because you've enjoyed hearing stories about your great-grandparents and wonder if similar stories were published; you circle "Stephen Crane" because you like *Maggie: A Girl of the Streets*; and you circle "social protest" because you have been involved in a protest for women's rights and you wonder about nineteenth-century women's movements.

Put each of these three or four new topics at the top of a separate page. Now make new lists under these topics in the same way as you made the first list. Your list on "Immigrant Literature" might look like this:

Ireland

Italy

1900–1915

community newspapers

novels, plays, short stories

discrimination

organizations

religion

By the time you have written these lists, you'll probably know which sub-topic excites you, such as "novels, plays, short stories." Narrow it down further—perhaps making another list—until you discover an idea that feels right to you. From the general topic, "American Literature Since 1865," you have come up with a topic that will really interest you, say "Stories by First Generation Italian-Americans—1900 to 1930." When you begin your research, you might narrow even further by choosing one writer to study in detail.

When You Have a Free Choice of Topic

If you are free to choose your own topic, make it a topic you feel passionate about. The choices are endless: The topic can be a field you have scholarly interest in; it can relate to your future career; it can be some offbeat subject you've always wanted to know about; or it can be in an area that will improve your life in some way. Any topic can become a subject for serious research. One writer, John McPhee, has made a career of writing books based upon research topics ranging from oranges to birchbark canoes. The topic is less important than your wholehearted commitment to study the subject inside and out, to live with it until you become an expert and can share your knowledge with others.

Here's a process to ensure that your topic means something important to you.

In a notebook, put each of the following questions on a separate page:

- What do I know something about?
- What do I want to know more about?
- What are my personal and professional goals?
- What challenges and problems do I face right now?
- What do I love?
- What makes me angry?

Now, as fast as you can and without stopping to think, list as many items under each topic as you can. Keep going until you get at least ten.

After you've put at least ten items on each of the six pages, go back and study each list carefully. Notice which of the items you feel most connected to. Circle the one item on each list that feels the most important to you. If you find that some of the same items appear on more than one list, that's a clue that the topics are important to you.

Suppose that several of your lists include references to trains and railroads. You've loved them since childhood. You collected model trains when you were little. And you are fascinated by your grandparents' stories about traveling on these old luxury trains.

You have just identified two narrowed-down topics about railroads— "Model Trains" and "Luxury Trains." For each of these, make a new and even more specific list of ideas. For example, your list about luxury trains might start like this:

grandparents' honeymoon

Santa Fe; Rock Island line

do these railroads still run?

treatment of black porters

Amtrak?

business—how luxury trains did financially

luxury trains—sleepers, pullman cars

famous trains—"The City of New Orleans," "Twentieth Century"

dining cars

sanitation—toilets?

You can see that the possibilities of topics related to railroads are unlimited—each a very specific topic. Railroad topics may be historical (the decline of passenger service in America), technical (computerized switching systems), or personally useful (planning a cross-country train trip you hope to take during summer vacation). You might end up investigating the story of one railroad company, or the toy train business, or refinements of diesel engines.

If You Get Stuck

If, after brainstorming, your lists are too short or nonexistent, try writing a list of everything you did or thought yesterday—just to get yourself going in the list-making mode. Then read this list for possible connections to a topic.

Another possibility is to have a friend look over your lists and discuss some possibilities with you. List any suggestions or questions your friend gives to you.

Freewriting to Explore Why Your Topic Matters

Freewriting, like brainstorming, is a chaotic, creative process. It is writing without any of the usual constraints, such as correctness and coherence. You write about your topic for a preset time, usually 10 to 20 minutes. In freewriting you write totally for yourself, you write without stopping to correct, you write whatever comes to mind (even if it does not always make sense), and you sometimes write one disjointed idea after another without transitions. Freewriting, in fact, is a lot like talking to yourself.

The big advantage to freewriting is that it gives you a shortcut to your best ideas. It gets you past your first view of the topic, which isn't necessarily your best approach. When you freewrite, you don't know what will come up. As you write without aim, your subconscious thoughts surface, often leading to surprises and breakthroughs. Twenty minutes of freewriting early in the project can save you from hours of writing in circles and starting over and over again.

Here are steps that will help you freewrite effectively about your topic:

Set a time limit.   Set aside 10 to 20 minutes by the clock and keep freewriting until the time is up. Commit yourself to this block of time no matter what.

Reflect briefly on your subject and then begin writing.   Write about why your subject is important to you. List everything you want to know about it.

Keep your pen moving.   Don't stop to think about spelling, to look up a word, to find the exact phrase you're seeking, or to evaluate what you have written. If your mind goes blank, write a simple word such as "stuck stuck stuck" or "and and and" over and over until a new thought comes to you. Keep freewriting until your time is completely up. The best material often comes right at the point where you think you've exhausted everything you have to say.

When your time is up, read what you've written.   Don't stop to edit or correct yet. Read what you've written with an open mind. Take special note when you feel surprised at something that popped out in your writing and mark it with an asterisk. At the bottom of the freewrite, write down a single sentence that sums up your most important point.

An Example of Freewriting

Here is a freewrite about the topic of "Stories by First Generation Italian-Americans—1900 to 1930":

Where did they live at first?

Wrote in Italian at first? Published? Where?

I don't know a thing about this topic. Why did I pick it? Maybe this is a mistake. All I know is that my grandmother told us great stories when I was little. She always said the Italian writers had heart—passion. They weren't wimpy. They wrote about blood & guts. But I've never read Italian writers. What intrigues me is what happened to this literary talent when they left Italy & came to this country. Did they write in Italian? Who published them? Who read their stories? When did they start writing in English? When did they start

using the hyphen—Italian-American? Did any of them achieve any fame? I

know about Mario Puzo, but he is too recent. I have to look into earlier ones.

Notice how the writer jumbles together ideas, worries, and questions in the order that they come to mind.

Searching for the Right Questions

Through brainstorming and freewriting, you've probably now hit on a topic that interests you. But if you proceed to the library with only a topic in mind, you might get lost in all the possible directions that topic could lead to. To save time and focus your search, you need a set of questions that you are trying to answer. In fact, you often can't find the correct answers until you've asked the right questions. Start now—in an ongoing process—to keep a list of questions about your topic. Select a section of your notebook for this purpose and add to it any new questions which occur to you as you conduct your research. Ask real and provocative questions. What really matters about this topic for you?

Let's say that your interest in railroads has led you to the topic of the rise and decline of passenger service on the Santa Fe Railroad. Here are some questions you might start with:

Why did the Santa Fe give up passenger service?

What were the peak years for this service?

Does the freight business today compare financially with the former passenger business?

Who started the company?

Who were their competitors, and how did they win out?

What men and women dominated the company?

What management style did their leaders use?

What innovations did the Santa Fe introduce?

Don't be too easily satisfied with your questions. As you get deeper into your research, keep looking for intriguing questions. Sometimes a new question opens a whole new way of looking at your topic. A famous example of how a single question can change the direction of a whole investigation occurred during the Senate Watergate hearings in 1973. Sam Dash, a Senate staff member, as an afterthought asked a simple question of Alexander

Butterfield, a White House aide, whether the President kept any tapes of his conversations. The answer that followed led directly to the resignation of President Nixon.

Defining Your Research Goals

As a final step before you plunge into the details, *write down your research goals.* Freewrite or make lists until you identify what you want to discover through your research. It's best to begin your research with a very specific idea of what you're after. For instance, if you chose first generation Italian-American writers as your topic, your goals might include:

To find some Italian-American authors who wrote fiction before 1930

To see what their stories showed about the lives of immigrants

To learn how and where the authors got published

To find out what became of them

As you prepare your list, one smart step would be to spend two hours in the library surveying the available sources and doing some general reading. This preview of your research will help you to choose goals that you can achieve. Your list of goals, in turn, will give you a definite sense of purpose at every stage of your project.

Chapter 3

Taking Advantage of Your Work Style

Now we come to a major factor in how you will approach any project—
your work style. To face an assignment effectively, you must first face yourself and own up to your actual patterns of work.

Deciphering Your Work Style

Here's an exercise that will help you analyze your workstyle:

Imagine that in two weeks you are going to visit a good friend for a
weekend at a college 150 miles away. Another friend is driving you,
you have money, you have arranged for time off, and you are free to
go. Spend several minutes imagining your preparations during the next
two weeks—from this moment until the time you put your suitcase
into your friend's car. Write a paragraph about what you would really
do. Don't write an idealized account of how you think you *ought* to
get ready; instead, describe how you actually *do* prepare for a trip out
of town. Use the following questions as a guide to write your account:

- When you plan for the trip, do you make lists and then check each
  item off? Or do you plan entirely in your head?

- Do you accomplish a few tasks each day or do you complete most
  of them on the last day?

- Do you stay with one plan or do you keep changing your plan as
  you go along?

- Do you discuss your preparations with friends or relatives and
  ask for their advice? Or do you work out most things for yourself?

- When it's time to go, how do you usually feel? As the time approaches, will you have everything completed? Are you ready early or do you have many details left to do at the last minute?

- Is this description typical of how you approach most projects?

Now write a paragraph in which you analyze your work style. If you're a procrastinator who puts off getting things together and ends up working under pressure, describe that style in detail. If you're a perfectionist who likes to be organized and in control, explain that style. If you combine these two styles, describe how that affects you. In your analysis of your work style, be certain to include any insights you gained about yourself from the exercise.

As you analyze your work style, don't be too critical of yourself. The exercise is designed to give you more understanding of how you work, not make you feel like a failure. Remember that a particular *result* may look the same to an outsider, regardless of the method that produced it. Some people get excellent results by putting themselves under last-minute pressure. They thrive on tension and excitement. Others don't like intensity and chaos, and prefer to work steadily and methodically over a longer period of time. What's important is to identify your own personal quirks and to make the most of your preferred work style.

Procrastinators and Perfectionists: What to Do About Your Work Style

No matter what your work style, there are advantages and disadvantages for each. Let's look at some strategies for capitalizing on the strengths of your work style and compensating for its weaknesses.

If You Are a Procrastinator

The advantages to procrastination are intensity, concentration, and a sense of adventure. The disadvantages are well known to all procrastinators and their families. A few short cuts for the chronic procrastinator follow:

Read "In a Crunch" Sections.   At the end of several chapters, we've included a special section for procrastinators. Although you should read the whole chapter, the last part has the time-savers you need at the eleventh hour.

Accept that you don't have the luxury of time.   Don't take on something you're not going to have time to do. For instance, you can't sit down and read a 400-page book on your topic if you have only two days to write the whole paper.

Learn to type and use a word processor. You lose at least a day—maybe days—if you must hunt and peck or get someone else to type. Nearly every college library has computer programs that teach typing and word processing. Word processing allows you to fix or change your writing without having to retype pages. A word processor or computer keyboard is basically a typewriter keyboard with extras. If you can type, you can use a word processor, and save yourself many tedious hours of typing time.

Survey your sources. Analyze which sources—books and people—can tell you the most. Ask experts, teachers, and librarians. Check a book's table of contents and index to zero-in on what you need.

Do at least one thing ahead of time. Pick one step that you don't mind too much and get it out of the way. Make one survey of the sources in the library, do one freewrite, or read one article. Pat yourself on the back for having accomplished one part of the job.

If You Are a Perfectionist

The great advantage of being thorough is that you have time to do a good job. The trick is to stay open, to let creativity bubble up, and to avoid filling time with unnecessary work. Here are some tips:

Don't let panic cloud your judgment. You can reduce a mountainous, overwhelming project to a series of manageable steps.

Don't organize or outline too soon. The purpose of research is to discover what you did not expect. You can hamper discovery by deciding too early what you will say or how you will organize your report. Instead, take advantage of your desire to start early. Allow the creative process to work for you by accepting a time of chaos while you gather ideas, talk to friends, survey possible sources, and "sleep on it" a while. During this process, keep a notebook handy so that scraps of information and ideas don't get lost.

Don't take too many notes. Notes aren't usable if they are voluminous. You should not try to copy down every word you read. Before you take *any* notes, look over your source for content. Not every source will pertain to your topic; it may have only one chapter that you want to examine. As you read, pause after each page to note the most important points or to jot down your own thoughts that the source has sparked.

Don't read every source or every word. Make sensible priorities about sources. How many will you need? How large a project should this be? For a two-page essay, reading six books might be silly; for a 200-page dissertation, six are not enough. Consider the time you can spend, survey the sources available, choose the best, and then let go of the others. As you read a book or article, be prepared to skim, looking for information pertinent to your topic. It is not necessary—not even advisable—to read every word.

Know when to quit.   A week before your deadline, you need to stop gathering information. Plan the final week, allowing more than enough time for consolidating your notes, deciding your focus, writing a rough draft, making changes, and typing your paper.

Collaborative Research: Working with a Team

Sometimes you will have an opportunity to collaborate on a research project. In college, you may be assigned a group project; in the professional world, your research will usually be as part of a team.

There are many advantages to collaboration. Sharing responsibility eases individual pressure; you can learn from others in your group; and you can balance each other's work styles. Collaboration is a great way to generate ideas or to incorporate several perspectives on a problem. In research, a team can discover more material than most individuals and can interpret that material from a variety of angles.

There are two different approaches to collaboration—either *strict division,* where each person is in charge of one aspect of the project from start to finish; or *shared responsibility,* where the team effort requires each member to be involved in virtually every aspect of the project.

Whether you volunteer to work with a friend or are assigned to work with a group, you should consider several points about how groups work most effectively:

Be open to the variety of ways different people contribute.   Some people like to take charge and immediately have an idea of what to do. Some are quiet but do excellent work. Some add fun and life to the process. Some care about getting details right. Some are eager to help with the basics—typing, for instance. At crunch time, the one who goes out to do the photocopying may be as much a lifesaver for the project as the one who finds the missing quotation.

Remember that negative criticism causes not only bad feelings but poorer work.   Avoid subdividing and back-biting. Also avoid being picky; often you will see that a problem which bothered you will get solved in the course of discussion. Stay positive toward each member of the group, give each person time to say what he or she thinks, and the group will work far more creatively, happily, and successfully.

Recognize that time "wasted" in exchanging news, having coffee, or arguing over the same point twice, is really not wasted. This process is how a group settles on its best ideas. It is also how more of the group becomes involved. To work well in a group, you need to tolerate some degree of chaos.

All three of these points add up to letting go of total control and exercising patience.

Some Tips for Working in a Group

Here are some practical steps that a group can take from the outset to ensure that they work smoothly and effectively:

- Use the power of group interaction. Meet regularly and frequently to exchange ideas and offer encouragement. Even when you have divided the project into individual responsibilities, plan on discussion and even some overlap. Take time to make sure that the group is functioning well—that no one is dominating and that no one is left out.

- Talk over how each group member works, and what each does best, and likes to do. Being aware of the team personality will help avoid the frustrations that can occur when the perfectionist is ready to outline and the procrastinator is still finding books.

- Allow the group to decide the division of labor. List all necessary steps and then let people volunteer for those they prefer or can handle best. Make sure that the group reviews the final list so that everyone feels that the division of work is both fair and practical.

- To avoid resentment, decide in advance how you will handle expenses and conflicts: How will you control photocopying costs? How will you make a decision if you reach an impasse? Find a solution that works for every person.

- Agree on deadlines when everyone will bring a certain amount of work to discuss. Even when you intend to divide the writing of the final report, seeing each other's work at key points will help you to unify the project and use everyone's ideas. Ideally, this feedback should occur at several intervals so that the plan can be adjusted as necessary. You can share your work in several ways: by reading notes or short passages aloud, by passing around each person's material for written comments, by photocopying all work so that each person has a copy, or by networking on computers.

- In most cases, write separately. The style and continuity are often disastrous when you compose sentences together. Revise as a group, but recognize that good revision takes time—through discussion, the group needs to talk until you all discover what you really want to say.

- Be flexible, ready to modify the original plan if it is not working. For example, one member may have been working harder and longer than anyone else with not much to show for it. When all the group members analyze the situation, they might decide that this person needs help or that this part of the project needs to be reconsidered.

Whether you work alone or in a group, be realistic about how you work and recognize that there are many different ways to get the job done.

Part Two

Becoming a True Researcher

Chapter 4

Sleuthing for Valuable Sources

Many of us enjoy watching or reading detective stories and trying to figure out clues; yet we rarely get the challenge of doing our own detective work. Research is detection: It takes a detective's persistence and flashes of insight. If you dread the prospect of research, one way to put energy into your work is to view research as "sleuthing" and to see yourself in the role of detective. Sleuthing means that you will check all the usual sources—in this case, books and reference works—and it also means that you will track down some surprising sources. One source leads you to other sources; one seemingly insignificant fact leads you to whole areas of investigation.

You might be tempted to begin your investigation at the library. Certainly that is where you'll find the most information under one roof; however, going to the library might not necessarily be your best first step. A better first step might be to assess all the information that is available to you right where you are.

For example, if you're in your home as you read this, you have at your fingertips one of the most valuable resources: the telephone book. So, we'll start with that and then look at other places both in and out of your home where you can find important, inexpensive, and unusual information.

The Telephone Book

You could spend a full day with the telephone book and not only enjoy yourself but find a lot of information that could turn out to be important to you. The *Yellow Pages* is also an excellent one-shot information source. Businesses and services in your area pay a great deal of money to get listed in the *Yellow Pages* just so people like you can easily find your way to them.

Here's how you can use the telephone book for your research project:

You can locate businesses that you can call or visit to get free brochures and other information. Suppose you're starting your research on a broad topic such as cruelty to animals. You can look in the yellow pages, get the phone numbers and addresses of local animal-rights organizations, and then call and visit them. Most organizations will give you free brochures and reprints of articles, surveys, and so forth, which, in turn, will aid you in getting a more specific focus for your topic.

You can also locate specific people who will grant you an interview, either over the telephone or in person. Many students have used the yellow pages to locate people to interview such as doctors, psychologists, directors of day-care centers, directors of sleep disorder laboratories, banquet directors, and so forth.

800 Telephone Numbers

Of course, 800 telephone numbers are not in the usual telephone book, although there are special 800 number directories. Or call 800 information (1-800-555-1212) and ask for listings of associations or companies that might offer brochures or information services related to your topic. Often you are able to get information over the phone and can list that source as an interview in your *Works Cited*.

Networking

Networking requires only that you let others in on what you want to know. It takes no other talent except perhaps the willingness to be energetically assertive. Tell your classmates, your friends, and all your relatives about your project and enlist their help in alerting you to source material.

Networking is as simple as opening your mouth and saying, "I'm conducting research on chess tournaments. Do you know anything about them?" Often people will answer, "No," but sometimes you'll get a response such as, "Actually I do. My brother won the intercollegiate chess championship in Utah last year." And even if they answer that they don't know anything whatsoever about chess, ask them if they can think of somebody else who might have information.

Also, anytime you talk to anyone about your topic, end the conversation by asking if that person knows someone else you could interview, or other sources of information you could explore. This easy question can end any conversation and will usually yield additional resources.

Query Letters

If there is enough time, you can write brief letters requesting information from specific organizations or individuals. This approach is especially useful if you cannot schedule a face-to-face interview. However, you must allow at least three or four weeks' lead time to get a reply. (Sometimes you can speed up the process with a telephone call.) Be certain to keep your query letter brief—never more than several paragraphs or one page. List the information you request item by item for ease in replying; limit your request to the essentials. Keep a copy of the letter for your records. Enclose a self-addressed, stamped envelope with your letter.

On-Site Visits

Make appointments with local businesses or institutions for an on-site visit. For example, if you're researching day-care centers, visit a day-care center and observe how it is run. If your topic is prison conditions, ask for a guided tour of a prison in your area. If you're researching an endangered species, visit your local wildlife museum or preserve. On-site visits are usually stimulating and can give you incentive to work on your paper in more depth. And don't be shy about asking. Most people are happy to take a break in their day and give information to others.

Institutions: Specialized Libraries, Museums, Historical Societies, and Organizational Headquarters

Check your local telephone directory for other repositories of information. Museums and non-profit organizations often have libraries open to the public. For example, in New York City, the American Kennel Club Library has materials on all registered breeds of dogs. The Old Court House Museum in Vicksburg, Mississippi, has an important collection of Civil War artifacts. The Whaling Museum in Sag Harbor, New York, has books and other information about whales and whaling.

Specialized Newsletters

Newsletters are another gold mine of information. There are newsletters for every kind of subject imaginable—writing, travel, food, and financial planning, to name a few. However, they're not always easy to track down and often you must pay a small amount for one issue, since newsletters are usually sold by subscription. However, associations and businesses will frequently give you a back-issue. (You might offer to pay postage for these.) Various departments within most big corporations generate several newsletters. The public relations office can tell you what newsletters are available.

Government Publications

As a citizen of a democracy, you have the right to a wide variety of information. Here are a few ways to learn what is available:

Call the Federal Information telephone number: 1-800-347-1997. Trained personnel will answer questions or direct your call elsewhere.

Call your congressional office. Your congressional representative maintains a staff, part of whose job is to provide information for constituents. These staff members know how to locate special government studies, reports of commissions, statistics, and other information that government departments gather. Congressional staff can help with topics of national or local interest.

Call other government offices. Your state representatives, your mayor's office, your county extension agent, and specific departments (Board of Education, Department of Consumer Affairs, Environmental Protection Agency, State Attorney General's office, and so forth) have information that is available to you. You can get a monthly catalog of publications on all sorts of topics—from farming to home construction—from the United States Government Printing Office in Washington, D.C. 20401 (202-512-0000) or from your library.

Visit your county courthouse. In the courthouse you can find the proceedings of court cases that deal with issues you may be investigating. In addition, you have the right to examine wills, deeds, and other public documents that provide valuable facts about people and places you may be studying.

Public Radio and Television

Public radio and television provide an amazing array of information on a variety of topics. Usually these topics are treated in depth on the news and talk programs. You can sometimes get transcripts of public radio or public television broadcasts—as well as some of the commercial networks' programs—usually for about ten dollars. Call your local station and ask—after you've found a specific program that interests you.

Videotapes

Videotapes are fast becoming a big source of information. Thanks to the rise in video stores and the ease of videotaping, you can now get a videotape on nearly any topic. Go to your local video store and check the index. Check daily television listings as well.

Other Visuals: Photographs, Illustrations, Movies, and Cartoons

The visual arts can provide historical evidence or commentary. You might need to photocopy some material for your appendix, but you can describe and interpret other material to prove a point. For example, the film *The Pawnbroker* shows how Spanish Harlem and other New York neighborhoods looked in 1967; Walker Evans's photographs show how many rural families lived in the South during the Depression.

Lectures and Talks

Another good source that you might overlook is notes that you've taken during class lectures or while attending a presentation. Be certain, however, that your notes are accurate and that any quotation you attribute to the speaker is exact.

Unusual Sources

Don't overlook the use of popular reference books such as *The Guinness Book of World Records* and *The Farmer's Almanac*. For example, the average American's daily water consumption could be a useful fact for a paper on water sanitation, or drought, or pollution, or hydroelectric power, or nutrition, or the flush toilet. Check the Appendix for a selected list of unusual sources.

A Tour of the Library

What It Is Called	What It Has
Catalogs	Computerized and card catalogs arranged by authors, titles, subjects
Reference Section	Reference desk, research librarians Reference books (noncirculating) include encyclopedias, dictionaries, bibliographies, and specialized references for various fields
Circulation Desk	Desk where books are checked out
Stacks	The shelves of books open to the public If "closed," a librarian gets the books for you
Periodicals Room (or Index Room)	Section where periodical indexes, databases, bound volumes and Holdings File (listing of periodicals carried by library) may be used
Microform Reading Room	Room where microfilm/microfiche are stored Machines for reading microform
Computer Lab	Section of the library housing computers which may be used Labs usually offer instruction
Vertical File	A file of clippings, pamphlets, and reprints of articles Ask a librarian for access
Media Lab (or Audio/Visual Lab)	Audio/visual equipment and films, records, CDs, tapes, and materials to accommodate disabilities
Reserve Room (or desk)	Location where teachers put on reserve materials for short-term use

Chapter 5

A Tour of the Library

You are probably familiar with your hometown library where you may have checked out your first library book. Hometown libraries are useful for having the best-known books and references and for local history and other topics of local concern. However, college libraries are preferable for research into most academic topics since they usually have larger collections and specialized periodicals. For some topics, you may even want to use a large university library or specialized research library.

Getting Around in the Library

If your college offers a course in research, by all means sign up for it. It usually carries college credit and will give you a solid foundation for all your studies. If you can't take a course in library research, however, the next best thing is to make friends with librarians. When you enter the library, head straight for a librarian or two and ask them where to start familiarizing yourself with the library. Most librarians are eager to help—that's exactly why they are there.

Next, take a quick walk around the entire library. Most libraries have a map of the floor plan. Pick one up and take it with you on your walk.

First take a look at three stations you will be using nearly every time you do research in the library:

- The catalog—whether on computers or on cards
- The circulation desk—where you check out books
- The reference desk—where you can get assistance

Computer Services

In addition to the main three stations, you should also know all the computer services available in the library. Computers have dramatically improved the process of locating materials. In fact, many materials will be available to you only via a computer monitor.

Catalogs   Most libraries now have their catalogs on computer programs.

Databases   Many databases (specialized references and listings) are now installed in computers that you can use. In addition, libraries also have access to other, huge databases that they can use to conduct a search for you—usually for a fee.

Programs   A large number of computer programs are available; many are already installed in the computers, ready to use.

Computer Lab   Most libraries have a section where you can use computers and word processors.

Finding Where Materials Are Stored

In order to find books and many other materials, your first step is to know your library's classification system.

Library Classification Systems

Library of Congress   Most colleges and universities use the Library of Congress classification system. In this system the call number begins with two letters of the alphabet. For example, *Pocahontas's Daughters: Gender and Ethnicity in American Culture* by Mary V. Dearborn has the following call number:

PS 147
.D 43

The Library of Congress system is divided into 21 major sections. "A," for example, is the designation for "General Works"; "P," for "Language and Literature"; and "Q," for "Science." The system is posted, as well as printed on flyers for you to take with you when you go to search for books.

The Dewey Decimal System   The Dewey Decimal System, used in most public libraries, divides books into ten major classes designated by number. For example, general works in this system is designated by "000," literature by "800," mathematics and the natural sciences by "500." Call numbers in this system begin with numbers rather than with letters. For example, *Pocahontas's Daughters* has the following call number:

$$810.992$$
$$.D$$

Locations of Materials

When you have some call numbers, you are ready to get the titles you have identified. Here are the locations of the books, periodicals, films, and electronic sources:

The Stacks   The "stacks" are the shelves that house all the books in the library that can be checked out. If the stacks are *open*, the book shelves are located on the floor of the library where you have direct access to them. If the stacks are *closed*, the shelves of books are located in a part of the library not open to the public. In that case, you have to fill out slips of paper to request books and wait until someone fetches the books for you.

Reference Books   Unlike the books in the stacks, which circulate and can be checked out for a period of time, the books in the reference section cannot be taken from the library. Books in this section are usually large publications, such as encyclopedias, dictionaries, and directories, or other books which contain a wide range of information, such as indexes, standard reference works, and bibliographies. (See pp. 35–36 and the appendix for a brief listing and description of some basic reference works.)

Magazines and Newspapers   Magazines, scholarly journals, and newspapers are housed in several ways: Current issues are in the periodical reading room—a separate location where you can take the current issue off the shelf and sit down to read it. Back issues of magazines and newspapers are kept in three separate locations: in their original format (for recent issues); bound into volumes and kept on the shelves in the reference book section; and on microform or CD-ROM. To see back issues—and to determine whether or not the library has these issues—you must consult the library's list of periodical holdings. To identify specific articles on your topic, you will need to consult an *index* (see pp. 42–43).

Pamphlets and Clippings   Pamphlets and clippings can provide valuable and unusual information, but these are often overlooked as a source, perhaps because they are not so easily accessible. To see pamphlets and clippings, you must ask where the library keeps its *vertical* or *clippings* files. These files are accumulations of pamphlets, articles, and brochures. Items are filed alphabetically but your topic may be filed under a more general category. For example, in one library William Faulkner may be given a separate file, while in another library he may be included in a general file under "American Authors." For help with locating materials in the vertical file, consult *The Vertical File Index*, a monthly publication that lists maps, posters, and articles under both subject and title.

Microform   To save space, libraries have many of their periodical holdings on film, which requires special equipment to read them. Instructions for use are printed on the machine. *Microform* is a term which includes microfilm (a reel of 35 mm film) and microfiche (a flat four-inch-by-six-inch sheet of film containing up to 96 pages of material). Before using microform, use periodical indexes to identify the articles that you want.

Films and Other Audiovisual Materials   Films, computer programs, recordings, tapes, and filmstrips are usually located in a separate section of the library. Here you may be able to watch films and listen to tapes and records or use computer programs. You can also find these materials through the library catalog.

Other Library Services

Reserve Room

Sometimes a teacher requests that materials for a specific class be kept in the reserve room. These materials are available for a shorter borrowing time than usual. Often they must be used in the library.

Book Request

If you cannot find a book in the stacks, ask at the circulation desk to see if the book is checked out or misplaced. If it is checked out, leave your name and the library will hold the book for you when it's returned.

Interlibrary Loan

If you identify a book or article that your library does not have, ask at the circulation desk for the person who handles interlibrary loan. The librarian can get the materials for you, often within days.

Services to Accommodate Disabilities

If you have need for materials in a special format (large print or audiotapes of print materials, closed-captioned videos, or adapted computers for physical limitations), the library has them or can help you request them. The *New York Times* has a limited edition each week in large print and the Kurzweill Reader electronically scans printed text and vocalizes the words. Adapted computers are new (and expensive), so your library may not have them, but volunteer organizations will tape printed materials for you or type your dictated material if you provide enough lead time.

Tracking Down Sources in the Library

To Use Reference Books	To Locate Books	To Locate Magazine and Newspaper Articles	To Locate Other Sources	To Locate Materials Not in Your Library
Go to the reference desk for help if you need it.	Go first to the computer catalog (usually located in the center of the library).	For current periodicals, go to the Reading Room.	For pamphlets, use pamphlet or vertical file.	Consult specialized bibliographies in reference section (see appendix).
Locate specific reference books in the computer catalog.	Do not use the *card* catalog (which is obsolete) except for specific purposes.	For all others, go first to the Periodicals Room.	For non-print materials (film, audiotapes, data disks, slides, etc.) go to media or audio-visual section.	Consult specialized periodical indexes and data bases in Periodicals Room.
Search through reference books on the shelves in the reference section. (Some may be located behind the reference desk.)	Locate the exact call number of the book by typing in author's name and title on the catalog.	Use the computer index catalogs.	For maps, posters, and artwork—ask at the circulation desk.	Consult *Books in Print* in reference section.
	Identify books on one subject by typing in several related subject headings.	For general articles, use the *Magazine Index Plus* and *The New York Times Index*.	For computer programs, go to the computer laboratory.	Consult bibliographies in recent books and articles.
	Using the call number, go to the stacks, get the book, and check out at circulation desk.	For specialized articles, see Appendix for a list of specialized indexes.	For specialized materials to accommodate disabilities, call in advance or consult a librarian.	Use interlibrary loan to request most valuable books and articles.
	If book is not on shelf: Check the reserve room. Ask at circulation desk.	Check bound indexes on shelves and tables: *The Reader's Guide to Periodical Literature*		If time and money permit, request a specialized search.
	If library does not have book, ask for it on interlibrary loan.	Specialized indexes		
		Check Holdings File to see if library carries the periodical.		
		Fill out slips for magazines to request copies. or		
		Go to bound volumes of periodicals on shelves or use periodicals on microform.		
		If library does not carry magazine, ask for article on interlibrary loan.		

Chapter 6

Tracking Down Books and Articles in the Library

Trips to the library are triumphs when they work, miseries when they don't. In this chapter, we give you some strategies for getting what you want from the library so that you won't have to leave frustrated and empty-handed.

Even if you're under a deadline, don't just rush pell-mell into the library and frantically grab anything you can find. Before you head for the library, make sure you have done the preliminary writing that will focus your search:

- Make lists to narrow your topic.
- Freewrite to discover your angle on the topic.
- Write down the questions you want to answer in your research.

For detailed help with these steps, see chapter 2.

These preliminary steps—the work of a few hours at most—will save you from wandering around the library, following irrelevant leads, and changing your topic half a dozen times. Instead, you will enter the library with a clear idea of what you want to find out.

Using a General Reference to Get an Overview

For many topics, a good place to start reading is the reference section of the library. Although your teacher may prohibit citing an encyclopedia or dictionary in the final version of your paper, reading an article in a general reference book will give you a quick overview of your topic.

As you read, make maximum use of your time in order to aim your research. Jot down key words that you might later look up as subtopics. Look also for specific suggested readings. Finally, consider your list of questions—your article may lead you to new, more precise questions to add to the list.

Here are some reference works to consider:

Encyclopedias and Dictionaries

For a general encyclopedia, *Encyclopaedia Britannica* is most often cited; for a general dictionary, *Webster's Unabridged* is most often cited. Be aware that the library also has many specialized encyclopedias and dictionaries (see the appendix, p. 187); you will find some of these listed in the library catalog.

Biographical Materials

For an initial overview of a person's life and work, you can start with *Who's Who*, which comes in a number of volumes corresponding to countries and professions, or with a biographical dictionary such as the *Dictionary of American Biography. The Biography and General Master Index* lists biographical articles located in a wide variety of sources.

Bibliographies

Volumes or computerized indexes, specific to each field, list books and articles in that field. Some are general (for instance, for literature, *The Modern Language Association Bibliography*, issued year by year); some, specific (for instance, *Eight American Authors*). Be sure to check the most recent copyright date of the bibliography to see whether it is current.

Specialized Reference Books

For a listing of reference books devoted to specific subject areas, see the appendix. For specific suggestions, consult the reference librarian.

Choosing Priorities for Selecting Sources

Before you sit down at a library computer to dig through listings, think through the kinds of sources that are best for your topic, your purpose, and your audience.

General Versus Specialized Sources

After getting an overview from a general reference work, you should move more deeply into your subject and farther away from this general beginning. You don't want to read the same basic information in six encyclopedias. Instead, move on to books and periodicals. You may find a book that includes a chapter on your specific topic, or you may find a whole book devoted to your topic.

On the other hand, some sources may be *too* specialized for you. For example, if you are studying gasoline additives, you will want to distinguish material written in plain English for the general public from material written in highly technical language by chemists for other chemists. It is useful to know that the term "magazine" is usual for periodicals written for the public, whereas the term "journal" is usual for periodicals written for specialists in the field. Within these categories is a wide range of styles and readability.

In choosing the level of your sources, consider also your reader's level of expertise. Are you writing for a specialist in the field? If so, you will want to move beyond general information into scholarly journals. But if you are writing for the general public or for a teacher not trained in your specific subject, you should rely more heavily on general or introductory sources.

Books Versus Periodicals

Your subject will determine how much you can rely on books as opposed to periodicals. For many subjects, you should use both. In general, current periodicals—newspapers, magazines, and journals—provide more recent information than books. Current information is necessary to produce good research—you want to reflect the latest findings in your field. But the more immediate the publication deadline, the less the chance for expert study and review. Think, for example, of a live news story on radio or television about a natural disaster; contrast it with the next morning's report; contrast those with the story in a weekly news report, then in a monthly magazine, and then in an end-of-the-year review. As the report moves from the date of the event, the author has time to consult experts, to study all angles of the event, and to eliminate bias and factual errors.

The time factor is even more relevant with books. Often, years of study and research precede the writing of a book. Nevertheless, books can't include the latest information, and much of the detail that is in magazines and newspapers never gets into books. Therefore, it's important to use a balance of both books and periodicals in researching most subjects.

Recent Versus Old Sources

Recent sources build on the sources of the past, so it is usually best to work from recent dates backwards through the periodical indexes and to begin studying the books with the latest copyright dates. Be aware of whether your source is out-of-date. Do not use a source from 1982 for a paper on current developments in computer design; do not quote someone saying "today" without making clear if the writer's today was fifty years ago.

However, there are two major exceptions to this rule:

Historical Topics   If you are researching from a historical perspective, you will want to use sources current at that time period. You may also want to use retrospective studies, so check periodicals dated around the fifth, tenth, fiftieth, or hundredth anniversaries (or other appropriate intervals).

Classics in the Field   These are often the first studies or landmark studies in a field. You can find these classics through careful reading; they will usually be referred to frequently in later studies. Be sure to consult these influential works.

Primary Versus Secondary Sources

Primary Sources   are written by the people actually involved in the subject you are studying. In a study of a novel, the novel itself is the primary source; so are any letters, notes, or memoirs the author has written. In a study of pioneer women, their diaries and letters are primary sources; so are county records of births, deaths, marriages and the like. In a study of Martin Luther King, Jr., his speeches and other writings are primary sources.

Secondary Sources   are written by people who, like you, are studying the subject. These writers rely upon primary sources. Secondary sources would include a critical study of a novel, a history of pioneer women, or a biography of Martin Luther King, Jr.

In many research projects, you will rely mainly on secondary sources. They are especially useful for providing the context surrounding primary sources. Nevertheless, as often as possible, go directly to the primary sources and draw your own conclusions.

Finding the Right Subject Headings

Many students trip and fall right at the start of their library work because they don't look under the correct heading. A student investigating English attitudes toward work may look under "England," but not under "Great Britain" or "United Kingdom." Or a student may look under "Work," but not under "Labor" or "Industry." The point is to be flexible and persistent.

Your freewriting, your list of questions, and your reading of a general reference source should yield a list of topics to search for. Go to the library prepared with a list of several headings to look up, and don't quit if one of them comes up blank. Here is where the librarian can be your best resource. Ask for help in identifying a fertile subject heading for your topic. The indispensable guide to locating subject headings is *The Library of Congress Sub-*

ject Headings, which lists nearly 200,000 headings that libraries use. Ask the librarian for the book and for help in using it.

As you search out information, consider how to narrow your topic. If you find hundreds of articles and books on your subject, look again at your freewriting to see what aspects you should be looking for. Suppose that the subject is "Roses." What is it that you want to know? You will begin your search very differently if you want to know about roses as plants as opposed to the rose as a literary symbol in literature.

Furthermore, looking up "roses" will yield far different information depending on which catalogs, indexes, or databases you use. Some listings will give very little; others will have exactly what you want. For example, in the general listings—the library catalog, *Reader's Guide to Periodical Literature, Magazine Index Plus,* and *The New York Times Index*—you will have to bypass books or articles on Pete Rose, The Rose Bowl, rose fever, and reviews of books and movies with "Rose" in their titles. If you want to study the rose as a commercial symbol, perhaps to learn how many roses are sold on Valentine's Day, consult business indexes (for example, *The Business Periodicals Index* or *The Wall Street Journal Index*). On the other hand, you will find articles about hybridization and pesticides developed for roses listed in *The General Science Index* or the *Monthly Catalog of U.S. Government Publications.* Within a specialized index or bibliography, look under several subject headings appropriate to that discipline—for example, "Hybridization" as well as "Roses."

If you are searching correctly, you should be narrowing down your idea of your topic. Your search should become progressively more specific.

Using the Library Catalogs

Libraries now list their holdings in computers. You can gain access to the information through the use of a video display and a keyboard. Many library computers have printers so that you can make a copy of the list of books you have found. Using the computer catalog is fairly simple; easy instructions are printed on the machine.

With the growing use of online catalogs, most card catalogs are obsolete. Libraries typically post a notice that reads something like, "No new entries since 1983. Please consult the computer listings for current holdings." However, if your subject field lends itself to older materials, or if the computer is down, you will probably find occasion to look through the card catalog.

Catalogs are arranged by three different listings, *author, title,* and *subject.* Within these headings, most computer systems allow the following commands (although the wording may vary):

Find Exact Title

The quickest way to find a single book is to type in the exact title, if you know it.

Find Title

Type in key words from a title to see the number of titles with those words. Type in **Display Brief** to see a complete, abbreviated list. You'll see a display that looks like this:

```
Your search:    FIND TITLE THE UPROOTED
Items found:    7 at NASSAU COMM. COLLEGE LIBRARY

1. Myer, Dillon Seymour, 1891- Uprooted Americans; the
   Japanese Americans and the War Relocation Authority
   during World War II . . .
2. Hindus, Maurice Gerschon, 1891- Humanity up-
   rooted, . . .
3. Holtz, Avraham. Isaac Dov Berkowitz; voice of the up-
   rooted. . . .
4. Handlin, Oscar, 1915- The uprooted. . . .
5. Handlin, Oscar, 1915- The uprooted; the epic story
   of the great migrations that made the American
   people. . . .
6. Coles, Robert. Uprooted children; the early life of mi-
   grant farm workers. . . .
7. Chekhov, Anton Pavlovich, 1860-1904. The bishop, and
   other stories, . . .
```

Note the number of the item you want to see. Then type in **Display Full** followed by the item number. (The full display will give you related subject headings that you can then enter to expand your search.) You will see a complete listing for each item, which looks like this:

```
AUTHOR          Handlin, Oscar, 1915-
TITLE           The uprooted; the epic story of the great
                migrations that made the American people.
PUBLICATION     [1st ed.] Boston, Little, Brown, 1951.
DESCRIPTION     310 p. 22 cm.
NOTES           ''An Atlantic Monthly Press book.''
                Bibliography included in ''Acknowledge-
                ments'' (p. 308-310) Library has Copies
                1-3.
```

SUBJECTS	1. Acculturation--United States.
	2. United States--Foreign populations.
CALL NUMBER	E184.A1 H27
LOCATION	Library

Find Author

Type in "Find Author," followed by the author's name. You will see the number of titles by that author in the library. Use the "Display Brief" command to see a listing of all the titles; then use the "Display Full" command to see a complete listing of each item you're interested in. Under an author's name you can also use the "Find Title" command—a useful procedure if you know only the author's last name and a word or two from the title.

Find Subject

Type in your main subject heading. If you find too many titles listed, type in two related subject headings connected by the word "and." You will see the number of books about both subjects available in the library. Type in "Display Brief" to see the number of books about those subjects. Choose the ones you wish to consult, note their item numbers, and type "Display Full," listing each item number. For instance, if you type in "Find Subject American Literature and Subject Minority," you could see this full display:

Your search:	FIND SUBJECT AMERICAN LITERATURE AND SUBJECT MINORITY AUTHORS
Items found:	2 at NASSAU COMM. COLLEGE LIBRARY
Item 1.	

AUTHOR	Dearborn, Mary V.
TITLE	Pocahontas's daughters : gender and ethnicity in American culture / Mary V. Dearborn.
PUBLICATION	New York : Oxford University Press, 1986.
DESCRIPTION	266 p. ; 22 cm.
NOTES	Includes index.
	Bibliography: p. 195-213.
SUBJECTS	1. American literature--Women authors--History and criticism.
	2. American literature--Minority authors--History and criticism. 3. Women in literature. 4. Minorities in litera-

ture. 5. Ethnic groups in literature. 6. Love stories, American--History and criticism. 7. Miscegenation in literature.

Now you could use the headings listed under "subjects" to continue your search.

No matter which command you use, be sure to type accurately; otherwise the computer will not know what you want. Once you have the display you want, use the printer (if available) to get a listing for each entry. This way you're certain to have an accurate record of each book for later use and the call number that you'll use to help you locate the book.

Using Periodical Indexes

To find a book, use the catalog; to find an article in a magazine or newspaper, use an *index*. A special section or room in your library houses many types of indexes. These indexes are kept primarily on computer and often in large volumes, usually one volume for each year, with subjects listed alphabetically. In either format—computer or book—you will need to try a variety of headings that fit your topic. Under each heading you will find a list of articles on that subject; in abbreviated form, each entry will tell you the title and date of the publication and the pages on which the article appears.

For instance, under the heading "Ethnicity," *Magazine Index Plus* for 1989–Dec 1992 (on computer) includes the following typical listing:

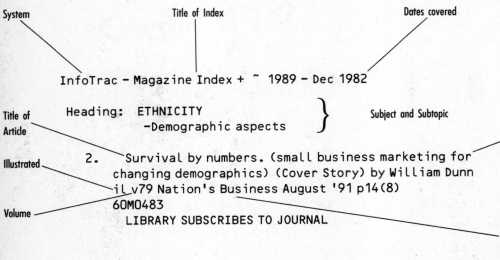

Here are some indexes with which you should be familiar:

Reader's Guide; Magazine Index Plus

Reader's Guide to Periodical Literature, and *Magazine Index Plus* cover articles from popular magazines written for the general public, such as *Newsweek, Popular Mechanics,* and *Psychology Today.* Such publications can give you an overview of your topic, contemporary reactions to an event, and feature articles related to your topic.

The New York Times Index; The National Newspaper Index

Since 1851, *The New York Times* has published annually an index of all subjects covered in the *Times.* This alphabetical list of subjects gives the title, date, section, page, and column for each article. *The National Newspaper Index* gives similar information about articles from other major newspapers.

These indexes are useful for recent information, since newspapers publish informative articles on science, international affairs, business, and other contemporary subjects. *The New York Times Index* is also useful for historical topics—guiding you to complete texts of major speeches, reports of battles and elections, reviews of performances, stock prices, box scores, and so forth.

Specialized Indexes

To find articles by experts on a specific topic, you will need to read scholarly journals. Articles in these journals are listed by subject in specialized indexes. For instance, *The MLA Bibliography* (published annually by the Modern Language Association) lists books and articles about literature. Here you can find articles on *Hamlet* by Shakespearean scholars. Such indexes exist in most fields: business, medicine, history, and so on. For a listing, see the Appendix.

When you have copied down or printed out a list of articles, next consult the *Holdings File* which lists the periodicals your library has. (The computer entry in some indexes will tell you whether or not the library carries the periodical.) Some of the articles in your list may be in periodicals that your library does not have. Before you copy down several titles from the same journal, make sure that your library carries that journal. If you need an article from a journal that your library does not carry, ask the librarian whether the article can be obtained on interlibrary loan.

Using Databases

Databases are computerized listings, sometimes of books and articles, sometimes of articles only. As with the library catalog and with periodical indexes, you will need to know what subject to look under.

Instructions for using the databases are printed on the computer, showing you the best way to phrase your query to get the most selective list of sources. For example, suppose that you are interested in the relationship between the novelist Henry James and his brother, the philosopher William James. Entering either name as subject in the database *Essay and General Literature Index* will give you a list of more than 400 works each—too many to know how to use. Entering both names connected by OR gives you a list of all works covering either of them—830. However, entering both names connected by *AND* gives you a list of 13 works. All 13 refer to both men.

Now, still using the database, you can examine the table of contents or "Subjects Covered" in each of the 13 works to see which you want to read. The list of subjects covered will also give you some new key words to enter as subjects for additional searches.

Be aware, as with indexes, that your library will have only some of the sources listed: be prepared to ask for interlibrary loan of an essential source.

For further advice on using databases in science, see chapter 19.

Using Your Sources' Sources

Some databases allow you to view the bibliographies of the books and articles listed to discover further sources. Look for repetition of certain sources: these may be "classics in the field" that you should consult.

You might also use a citation index—*Arts and Humanities Citation Index, Science Citation Index,* or *Social Sciences Citation Index.* These list not only what subjects were written about in a given year but also which older articles were referred to in other articles that year.

Allowing Time for Browsing

After you've gathered some titles and call numbers from the card catalog, go to the general section and browse through the books on the shelf. Sometimes you will find a valuable book on the same shelf as others that you found through the catalog. Check the backs of a number of books for *bibliographies*—listings of other books in the field. Allow yourself some time to browse, not only through the books on the shelf but also through current magazines and periodicals. When you are concentrating on a particular subject, an amazing event happens: Current articles seem to leap out at you. It often seems that others are discovering the subject right along with you.

How to Assess a Book or an Article

A Book

Before you start reading a book, you need to evaluate what it has and does not have for you. Check its date by looking at the back of the title page; depending on your topic, you may need up-to-date information. Several parts of the book can tell you quickly if it will meet your needs. Start with the table of contents: Does the book have chapters that relate directly to your angle? Look in the index under headings of special concern to you. Read the jacket material and author's biography (back cover or back pages). Finally, look at the preface or introduction. See how the author presents the purpose of the book. The preface may point you to other important books; the introduction may give you an overview of the topic. Now you are ready either to read specific sections of the book or to set it aside for the librarian to re-shelve.

An Article

In looking over an article, the first consideration is level of sophistication and readability. Depending on your background and the level of the course for which you are writing, you may reject an article that seems simplistic or one that is too technical. Also, distinguish between articles that *explain* a subject as opposed to feature articles that tell about a person or an incident related to the subject. An article about a restaurant in Princeton where Einstein liked to eat is not normally relevant to a study of his scientific ideas.

Problems

When you can't find any book on your subject: Don't give up. Look under all possible related subject headings. Check the reference section of the library for more general sources—look at indexes, bibliographies, and so forth. If all else fails, *ask the librarian for help*—always your most important emergency tactic.

When the book is not on the shelf: If there's time, ask the circulation desk to reserve the book for you when it is returned or see if it is available through interlibrary loan. However, the book may be in the library, but in use or improperly shelved. Look among neighboring books in case it is misplaced. Check with the librarian to see if it is on reserve, or check the shelf again before you leave.

When you find too many books: Reconsider your subject heading. Can you narrow it? You may be able to eliminate many of the books by their titles (either too general or too restrictive) or by their dates. Check the most recent first. Ask a teacher or other experts in the field which are the most valuable books. And, remember, the preface and acknowledgements of recent books may refer to classics in the field.

When the periodical is not in the Holdings File: If there's time, ask the librarian to arrange for an interlibrary loan of the article.

In a Crunch

Working in the library, especially if you are under a tight deadline, can be overwhelming. Here is a sequence of steps you can follow when you're in a crunch:

Use the charts on pages 28 and 34.   These charts will give you a quick overview of the library.

Stay open to discovery.   No matter how tight your deadline, allow yourself a small chunk of time to browse and get ideas before making your first move.

Jot down the questions you want to answer.   You can't research well if you can't find some point of interest to start from. Taking a few minutes to prepare a list of questions will give you a clear direction. Be sure to check that list before you leave the library to make sure you haven't forgotten any essential information.

Start with a reference book.   An encyclopedia or specialized reference in the field can give you a quick overview and help you to further identify your topic.

Enlist the librarian's help.   Admit the deadline you are under. Describe the restrictions of the assignment and what topic you are considering. Ask for one or two suggestions.

Locate some recent articles.   Read the most recent information you can find—usually in magazines or newspapers. (Consult periodical indexes.) Such articles will give you useful information and lead you to other sources.

Assess the available sources in the library.   After checking to see what is available in the library, modify your topic accordingly. Use whatever material you can get your hands on immediately. Given this available information, what can you write about? What aspect most interests you at this point?

Don't stop to read and take notes in detail.   Look quickly to see if a source is useful. Examine the table of contents and the index, or skim a chapter.

Photocopy material to use later.   Rather than stopping to take notes, photocopy pages that attract your attention. Caution: Make sure that you write down all the bibliographical information on photocopied material and make sure that each page number is legible.

Gather a few extra sources.   Grab another two or three books or articles. You'll probably find a use for them later—especially if you're in a pinch.

Chapter 7

Taking Notes and Taking Stock

You've got a stack of books and articles that look relevant to your topic and you're ready to start gathering information. At this point, you need a strong sense of what you are looking for; otherwise you will waste hours reading and jotting down information you cannot use, or you will end up writing a paper that is all over the place.

To maintain a sense of purpose and to move forward efficiently, get out the list of questions you formulated before you went to the library. As you dig into each book or article, ask yourself whether it is relevant to your particular approach to the topic. Look for new questions to add to your list—or new ways to formulate the key questions.

As you read, consider whether the article merely repeats what you've already found, and whether the information is out-of-date. Look for those statements and facts that either will back up your own ideas or that challenge you to modify them. This way you won't get bogged down copying every fact you come across: You will have an eye out for the facts you can actually use.

Keep a Working Bibliography

The moment you even touch a book or magazine, stop and write down the following information:

Book	Magazine or Newspaper Article
• author—last name first	• author
• title of book	• title of article

(continued)

Book	Magazine or Newspaper Article *(continued)*
• city of publication • publisher • year of publication	• title of periodical • date • section, if any • page numbers • volume number for scholarly journals

Occasionally you will need additional information: editor or translator; author, title, and pages of an article in a book; volume number of a book in a series.

The bibliographical information for *Coming of Age in the Milky Way* by Timothy Ferris would be:

Ferris, Timothy. Coming of Age in the Milky Way. New York:

Doubleday, 1988.

Keep your bibliographical notes in a separate place, preferably on notecards, filed by author. This is your *working bibliography*. When it's time to type a bibliography or a works-cited page, all you have to do is alphabetize your sources, making a sometimes difficult task quite easy. Be sure to arrange the bibliographical information in the correct format to prevent problems later (see chapter 15 for specific directions). A further good idea is to put under each bibliographical entry a brief *précis note,* a sentence or two that summarizes the book or article. Here is a précis note for *Coming of Age in the Milky Way*:

> This book traces the development of theories of the universe. It covers the ideas of great scientists starting with the Greeks. It has an appendix, a glossary, a brief history of the universe, and a bibliography.

Even if you think the source won't fit into your project, the précis note will be useful as a reminder when you review your sources.

Don't Confuse Note-taking with Writing a Paper

You cannot write your paper as you read your sources without committing plagiarism and creating a disaster. *First* take your notes; *then* write a first draft of your paper without looking at your notes. Later go back and add specific information along with the proper documentation. Following this sequence will help you avoid the pitfall of copying or rewording blocks of material and presenting them as your paper.

Read Selectively and Critically

Too often students accept any published writing as gospel. Rather, you need to read with a little skepticism. Just because something is in print doesn't necessarily mean it's true. Writers are people: They have their own angle and their own ideas of how to pull the topic together. In other words, they have their own slant on the subject.

For instance, suppose you are writing about Vietnam veterans. As you read each book or article, ask whether the writer is a veteran or not, whether the writer believes the war was necessary or not, whether the writer is a psychologist, historian, sociologist, or journalist. The answers will affect how you interpret what you read.

When to Take Notes

Don't take notes the minute you set foot in the library. Instead, take time to survey the available sources before you plunge in. Similarly, don't decide in advance what you're going to say in your paper. Stay open to discovery.

Here are some signals for recognizing a valuable note:

When you find yourself very interested in a particular point.   You might even hear yourself saying, "Well, that's interesting. I didn't know that." If so, make a note.

When you feel your temper rising.   If you encounter material that's contrary to your point of view, make a note. This kind of material gives you a point to argue against.

When you run across a particularly effective statement.   Write it down word-for-word to quote in your essay. Be certain to record who said or wrote it and the title of the work. Include the *exact* page number.

When you find any statement, information, or idea that supports your own position.   Make it a point to look for—and record—information that proves your own position.

When a source seems useless.   Even though you took no notes from it, write at least one sentence or two to sum it up. You may later find a use for that summary—especially if you are short of sources.

Four Ways to Take Notes

You probably already have some kind of note-taking method. But different occasions require different types of notetaking. It helps to know how to take notes in more than one way. The four most common ways to take notes are

- in a notebook
- on notecards
- onto a typewriter or computer
- directly onto photocopied material

Each of these has advantages.

1. A Notebook

The advantage of notebooks is that they keep material in sequence. The disadvantage of a spiral notebook is that you can't move the notes into clusters. Instead of a spiral, use a looseleaf notebook or folders.

Here are some tips for taking notes in a notebook:

- Write the author and title at the top of a notebook page, along with information for your bibliography.
- Before you jot down a note, write in the left margin the number of the page you are reading—to use later when you give credit to your source. Do this no matter what you are noting—an idea, a fact, or an exact quotation.
- Keep a separate page—or pages—for each source. Also keep a section of pages for your own ideas, to capture them as they occur to you. Write on one side of the page only so that you can cut and rearrange the material later if you want to.
- In the front of your notebook or folder, keep a list, in order, of the sources you cover in that notebook.

2. Notecards

Notecards are an efficient way to take notes because you can easily shuffle the notes into your paper and alphabetize your sources.

Here's how to use notecards:

- Put the author's last name at the top of the card. That's the only identification you will need as to the note's source. Obviously, if you have more than one book by an author, you must indicate with a key word the title of the book. If there's no author, use the first few words of the title.
- Write down only one item per card: one idea, one quotation, one passage, one fact.

- Write down the exact page number where you found the item.

- In the top right-hand corner, write *in pencil* what you consider the main topic of this information. Use pencil so that you can change your topic as you go along.

- Keep a separate section (using a small file box really keeps you organized) where you put your own ideas, questions, and so forth as you go along.

- When you have all your notes on cards, separate them into piles according to the same topic you've put in the right-hand corner. This method will get you a head start in organizing your paper.

3. The Computer or Typewriter

You can transfer notes from your sources directly onto the computer or typewriter. In some cases you may be able to transfer quotations and documentation directly into your paper. This method can save you time. However, the big danger exists that you might construct your paper out of chunks from your sources instead of stressing your own ideas.

As with a notebook, be certain that you record complete bibliographical data and the page number of all notes. Also, keep a separate section or use a special tag (such as "my idea") for your own thoughts.

4. Photocopies

Sometimes a page filled with information is best photocopied. Then you can highlight or underline precise data for use in your paper.

The advantage of this method is that you can be absolutely sure that you have accurate statistics or direct quotations. The disadvantage is that photocopied material is unwieldy compared to notecards or notebooks—and it is not in your own words. Therefore, you will need to incorporate it into your own style (see chapter 11).

Before you return the source from which you photocopied, be sure to write *onto the photocopy* all bibliographical data. Also make sure that page numbers are legible.

When to Photocopy

— When a page is dense with facts or technical language
— When a page contains statistics, tables, graphs, or charts you will reproduce in your appendix

— When a page has one or more important extended quotations
— When you come across a bibliography with several sources you
want to check

When to Save Your Money

Don't photocopy a page containing only one or two useful points. Jot them
down in your own words.

How to Take Good Notes

Good notes are a mix of various kinds of information.

Take notes almost entirely in your own words.　Use summary and
paraphrase rather than mostly direct quotation. Quote only key phrases and
facts.

Use some direct quotations.　Direct quotations are not just something
spoken by another person; they are also any words *written* by another person. Be absolutely vigilant in putting quotation marks around every word
that you take from your sources. If the writer quotes someone else, be sure
to note who is being quoted—and the source of the quote. Also, don't
overdo using direct quotations. Keep them to no more than 25 percent of
your notes.

Get your facts straight.　Any statistics and facts must be recorded accurately. Take special care to copy all numbers, names, and other facts correctly.

Keep each note brief but clear.　Be sure that each note will make sense
to you when you read it later.

**Write down your own comments, ideas, and questions as you think of
them.**　Distinguish your own ideas from those of your source by indicating with a tag such as "my idea."

**Keep an accurate record beside each note of the source and the exact
page number.**　If the note covers material that runs more than one page,
indicate for yourself where the page changes. This habit will ensure that
your documentation is fully accurate.

An Example of Note-taking

Suppose that you are studying the debates among the scientists who developed the atomic bomb. You already know, in general, the main historical
events and the basics of how the bomb worked. Now you are taking notes

on Timothy Ferris's *Coming of Age in the Milky Way* (1988). Here is one paragraph from page 252 of the book:

> When nuclear fission, the production of energy by splitting nuclei, was detailed by the German chemists Otto Hahn and Fritz Strassmann in 1938, and nuclear fusion, which releases energy by combining nuclei, was identified by the American physicist Hans Bethe the following year, humankind could at last behold the mechanism that powers the sun and the other stars. In the general flush of triumph, few paid attention to the dismaying possibility that such overwhelming power might be set loose with violent intent on the little earth. Einstein, for one, assumed that it would be impossible to make a fission bomb; he compared the problem of inducing a chain reaction to trying to shoot birds at night in a place where there are very few birds. He lived to learn that he was wrong. The first fission (or "atomic") bomb was detonated in New Mexico on July 16, 1945, and two more were dropped on the cities of Hiroshima and Nagasaki a few weeks later. The first fusion (or "hydrogen") bomb, so powerful that it employed a fission weapon as but its detonator, was exploded in the Marshall Islands on November 1, 1952.

Ferris, Timothy. *Coming of Age in the Milky Way*. New York: Doubleday, 1988.

Following are notes you might take, bearing in mind your interest in the scientific debates that preceded the atomic bomb:

Ferris, *Coming of Age*

252   Einstein doubted possibility of fission bomb—"inducing a chain reaction" compared to "trying to shoot birds at night in a place where there are very few birds" (Ferris's wording)

7/16/45—first fission bomb—detonated, New Mexico

Note to myself: Get dates of Hiroshima, Nagasaki

The notes you take depend on your topic. If you were studying the early stages of the hydrogen bomb, you probably would not note Einstein's comment; instead, perhaps you would note the following different information:

252   Hans Bethe, American—identified fusion, 1939

        fusion—"humankind could at last behold the mechanism that powers

        the sun and other stars" (Ferris)

        11/1/52 Marshall Islands—first H-bomb—used "fission weapon" for

        detonator

These notes are focused on your specific topic, they are brief but precise, they are clear about who said what, and they include the page number.

Flashes of Inspiration

Take time frequently during your research to stop and write down your own ideas and reactions. These notes will be extremely valuable later when you're looking for the proper angle for your paper. Remember that your final paper will be largely *your* thoughts—not just chunks of information from your sources. *You* will supply the emphasis, the order of points, the introduction, the evaluations of sources, and the conclusions. If you wait until you're "ready" to write the paper, you may find that your ideas have flown.

Therefore, seize all good ideas that come to you while you're reading sources—or even while you're on the way home from the library. Stop and write them down immediately.

Do not shortchange your ideas when they come. Write them out in sentences and paragraphs, and you will find that when you sit down to write your paper, some of it is already in a good first draft.

Taking Stock

After you have gathered your notes together, you need to survey them and to begin the transition that culminates in a paper built upon your ideas, judgments, and conclusions. Now is the time to define your own angle on the topic.

As you read all your notes, highlight or mark important ideas, facts, and quotations.   At the same time, keep a page at hand for writing any flashes of inspiration about your plan for the paper.

Be selective.   Sort out what you will use and what you will set aside.

Save all your notes.   Don't throw away any notes until the project is over. Toss them into a box and save them just in case.

Set your notes aside and write—from memory—what they add up to. Write in any order for 20 minutes or more. What do you remember from all these notes? What is important? What might you stress in your paper? How do you imagine the shape and style of this paper? What will it accomplish? This freewriting will help you to figure out your priorities for the paper.

Chapter 8

Conducting an Interview

One of the swiftest and most enjoyable ways to gather information on a particular subject is to interview a prominent figure or a professional in the field. This person can be an author of books or articles you've read, someone who has been mentioned in the material you've read, or simply someone you know of. Just be certain that the person you choose has firsthand experience with the topic you're researching.

If you can't immediately think of someone you'd like to interview, ask around and collect some names and phone numbers. Then begin calling and checking out the possibilities. This process takes time, so start at least three or four weeks ahead to give yourself plenty of lead time.

At first you might feel intimidated about calling someone important and thus too busy to grant an interview. Actually, most people like to be interviewed and, if you're persistent and use good sense and good manners, chances are that you can get an interview with almost anybody you set your heart on.

How to Get an Interview with Almost Anyone

Pinpoint exactly the person you'd like to interview.

Spend time and energy pinpointing exactly the person you'd most like to interview and precisely what you want to find out from him or her. This information should not be easily available in printed form. Let's say that you have seen Amanda Ellis on a television program discussing her views on the outrageous cost of producing music videos. She herself has produced them and has also written an article about music videos—which you have already found and read. Ms. Ellis also happens to live in your area.

Write a telephone script.

Before telephoning her, take a few moments to write out a "script," which is the equivalent of a sales pitch. Write out exactly, in one sentence, why you want to interview Ms. Ellis and be prepared to state it—and explain it, if need be—as quickly as possible. You then track down her phone number and call a few weeks in advance to request an interview. Often a number of phone transactions are involved in this step, so don't get discouraged.

Be persistent.

When you call, you are apt to reach an assistant. Give your name, explain that you are a student doing research (many people will help students before they will help other professionals), and say that you are calling to request an interview with Ms. Ellis. With your script in front of you, deliver your one-sentence request. Emphasize that you are willing to settle for even fifteen minutes (once you get in the door, you will nearly always get more time than you asked for). Be polite, but don't be too quick to take "no" for an answer. Keep negotiating until you see an opening. Keep calling back if necessary. At all times, make it a point to use excellent telephone etiquette: identify yourself clearly, state emphatically what your goal is, and act confident—as if you expect to have your request for an interview met.

Get the interview and set a date.

Set a date as soon as possible. Often dates have to be changed, so stay flexible, but definitely try to complete your interview a week ahead of your deadline. If you reach an answering machine, leave your name and phone number first and then briefly explain what it is you want. Be doggedly persistent. Do not give up until you get an appointment for a specific date.

Before the Interview: Doing Your Homework

Find out all you can about your interviewee.

Before you show up at the interview, find out as much as you can about Ms. Ellis. Ask her assistant for information; check biographical collections for capsule accounts of her life and career; see if there have been articles written about her. Knowing something about her ahead of time will both compliment her and enrich the interview for both of you. Also, having this information in advance will save time by reducing routine questions. It will also give her a feeling of confidence in you; she'll see that you're serious enough to have done some homework. In other words, you are there for a constructive purpose and not to waste her time.

Go in as an expert on your subject.

In addition to the material you've gathered on her, review other material you've read on your subject so that you are as knowledgeable as possible. This expertise will enable you to lead Ms. Ellis into areas of special interest to you.

Formulating Questions for the Interview

Well before the interview, prepare a list of questions you want answered. Arrange them in order of priority—the most important first and so on. This way, should the interview get cut short, she will have answered your major questions.

Keep your questions few and specific—no more than eight to twelve. You want to leave time in the interview for easy conversation between the two of you. Sometimes that's when the most exciting information happens—when you are just talking.

Never ask a question that can be answered simply with a "yes" or "no." Closed questions could result in zero information. Ask questions that demand a thoughtful response and give her time to think before she responds.

Here's a suggested sequence for your questions:

Background Begin with only one or two questions that will fill in your knowledge about Ms. Ellis's background and experiences, something like, "How did you first get interested in this business?" These questions can be about her education, her job experiences, what she currently does professionally, and so forth. Keep this part brief.

Major Topic Be certain that you formulate *one* major question that you want her to answer. Make it simple and direct. In your interview with Ms. Ellis, you might ask, "What exactly makes music videos so expensive to produce?" Then let her talk. Remember that this question is the main reason for the interview.

Compose two to four follow-up questions related to the main topic—just in case you need them. For example, after Ms. Ellis has answered your main question, if she hasn't covered certain information, you could ask her, "What is the single most expensive cost item in producing a music video?" or "What steps do you take to control costs?"

Minor Topics Prepare two or three questions about other points you'd like to explore, but use them only if you have extra time. Sometimes this information can be useful and exciting. Just be careful not to get off the track. If time permits, you could question Ms. Ellis in an area of special interest, such as, "How do you get started if you want to become a producer of music videos?" or "What plans do you have for upcoming videos?"

Problems/Solutions Near the end of the interview, find out the major problem that bothers Ms. Ellis about this field. What makes her blood boil? What ax does she have to grind? This question is basically two-part. Simply ask her, "What do you think is the biggest problem in this field?" After she's described the problem, then ask, "What do you think are some possible solutions to this problem?"

Final Questions Before the interview ends, plan to ask two final questions:

- "Can you recommend other resources besides yourself—books, articles, people?"

- "I'm a beginner in this field. Are there any other questions I should be asking?"

As your interview date approaches, group your questions in the order in which you will ask them. Write them down on a pad to take with you for the interview. Check again to be sure none can be answered with a simple "yes" or "no" and also be sure that you have arranged them in order of priority. You should now have a short list of eight to twelve simple questions written on a pad all ready for your interview session with Ms. Ellis.

During the Interview: Keeping the Lead

Tape record the interview if possible.

Recording the interview will take pressure off you and will keep you more relaxed during the interview itself. Instead of worrying about writing down everything or feeling anxious that you might forget important information, you'll be free to concentrate on the conversation between you and Ms. Ellis.

If you're going to tape record the interview, take care of *two* preliminary steps: Ask permission ahead of time—most people will say yes—and make sure that your machine is in good working order. Use batteries whenever possible to eliminate worries about where to plug in, but be certain the batteries are fresh and will last through the interview.

Listen far more than you talk.

The first and foremost rule for conducting a successful interview is to be a good listener. Get Ms. Ellis talking and your job will be easy. Don't be afraid of silences. Relax and give her thinking space. Don't jump in every time there's a pause.

Take notes.

Even if you tape record the interview, take brief notes during the interview as a record of the *sequence* of the conversation. This record will be useful later when you are trying to locate specific spots on the tape.

If you don't tape record the interview, taking notes is essential and you will have to write down more information. However, don't let writing distract you so much that you seem more preoccupied with taking notes than listening to what Ms. Ellis is saying. *Keep your notes brief* and simple. Leave plenty of space around each note so that you can go back and insert further information after the interview. If you find later that you are missing an essential piece of information, call and ask for it.

Take down plenty of good direct quotations.

Write down plenty of good direct quotations so you can capture on paper the flavor of Ms. Ellis's way of speaking. It's okay to ask her to repeat something she said or even to go back to something you didn't quite get a few moments ago. Doing so shows her that you intend to be accurate when quoting her.

Allow some creative thinking time.

Let Ms. Ellis stray from the questions a little because this often leads to surprising information. If, however, the time begins to run out, steer her back to your questions so you can get most of them answered. Remember that conversations are not linear—people skip around.

Probe.

If you feel Ms. Ellis has some emotion going in a particular area, ask some spontaneous questions that will uncover unexpected insights.

Add your own comments throughout the interview.

During the interview, feel free to insert your own insights and opinions, especially when based on prior research you've done. Your comments will show her that you've done your homework and that you consider yourself a budding professional in her field. She may even turn out to be a valuable contact for you if she's impressed with the way you've handled yourself during the interview.

Remember to ask the problem/solution question.

Near the end of the interview, ask Ms. Ellis the problem question. Ask it directly and simply: "What do you think is the biggest problem in this field?"

Do not "lead" this question; that is, don't indicate what *you* think is the biggest problem. If she can't think of something, keep probing. Ask further, "What upsets you most?" Be alert. Feed her back some of the information and ideas she has already given you. After she's stated and discussed the problem, ask her, "What do you think are some possible solutions?" That's all you need to say. Let her take it from there.

Take charge of ending the interview.

Don't wait for Ms. Ellis to end the interview. Once you feel she has answered most of your questions, make an efficient exit. Indicate that you are ending the interview by standing up, thanking her, and shaking hands. Tell her how much you enjoyed the interview and how much you appreciate her giving you so much time and attention. Ask her if you may call her and clarify a few points should that become necessary.

After the Interview: Getting It Down on Paper

Immediately after the interview, jot down some notes giving your evaluation of the interview, your impressions of Ms. Ellis, and the most important piece of information you obtained.

When you arrive home, write or type additional notes. If you taped the interview, listen to the tape and make notes. Write down your impressions of Ms. Ellis. Include dialogue or quotations, trying to quote her as accurately as possible. Leave plenty of white space so you can go back and add things you later remember. At this point, if you're unsure of some things or need additional information, call Ms. Ellis for clarification of a few points, emphasizing that you don't want to misrepresent her.

Now, before you forget about it, write Ms. Ellis a note thanking her for her time and interest. Offer to send her a copy of your final paper if that seems appropriate.

Some Pitfalls to Avoid

- Asking yes or no questions
- Asking too many personal questions—a professional interview is *not* about someone's personal history.
- Asking too many lightweight questions
- Failing to emphasize one major question which will yield the most information.

For suggestions for writing a report of your interview, see chapter 21.

In a Crunch

If you fail to locate the right person for an interview or fail to obtain a satisfactory one, take these steps in a crunch:

- Ask parents, your teacher, or classmates if they know someone appropriate who might grant an interview.

- Interview a professor or counselor who is on your college campus. These knowledgeable people are usually readily available and happy to share their expertise.

- Use the telephone yellow pages and call authorities on your topic until you locate one near you.

- If you can't uncover a single person who has time for an interview, request a telephone interview. This approach is far better than coming up with nothing.

- If your interview failed to gather sufficient information, you can either find an alternate interviewee or call the first person you interviewed and get additional information over the telephone.

Part Three

Putting Yourself on the Line: Reporting What You Have Found

Chapter 9

Making a Plan: Taming Your Information

A helpful metaphor to explain the next stage is to think of everyone in the class being given a surprise box full of objects. The boxes will all contain the same objects; but the challenge is for each person to use these objects to make something different. You could assemble them in a variety of ways depending on your imagination. Think about the different sculptures—or bookcases or tables—you could make out of seven one-by-sixes and a box of screws. Similarly, everyone in class could make a different patchwork quilt given the same scraps of fabric. Everyone could make a different meal given the same groceries.

Your challenge as a writer is similar. You've collected all sorts of information and ideas. You have a "box" full of notes. Now you have to decide what to share with the reader. Are you going to just hand the reader the box? You need to make some decisions, and the way you make decisions is to discover what matters most to you about your research. Then you can build your notes into a unified paper with a clear progression of ideas.

Discovering the Emphasis of Your Paper

Now comes that sinking feeling. You've done all this research and now you have to transform it into a coherent paper. But how do you get started? How do you find an angle for your paper, an angle that really matters to you?

Freewriting is the way to begin. You've collected and digested a large amount of information. Now, through the process of freewriting, you will uncover what you think about all this information. You will discover your own viewpoint.

Set your books and notes aside; don't refer to them at all during the free-write. Get out some fresh paper. Set a timer for twenty minutes. Begin writing immediately and write without any long pauses. *Your purpose is to decide what is important in the material you've found.* Do not stop writing until the full twenty minutes is over. If you run dry, reread what you've written and expand upon one of your points.

Here are two questions to keep in mind as you freewrite:

– How does what I've learned tie in with what I thought when I started?

– Out of all I've learned, what is most important?

After you've finished freewriting, go back and underline the most important sentences—the ones that seem to contain your strongest opinions, feelings, and attitudes. Be on the lookout for sentences that echo each other and say the same thing in different ways. Write down these important sentences on a separate sheet of paper and reflect on them for a few moments.

Developing a Central Statement

Once you have isolated some good ideas, you're ready to try writing a *central statement*—sometimes called a thesis sentence—that will control your whole paper. Read over your freewriting and underline the best points. Then write *one sentence that says what your paper will prove.* Try several versions of this statement to find the best expression.

If you're still unsure of your central statement, ask yourself what you want to emphasize above all in your paper. Write your answer in one strong sentence: "The major point I am trying to make in this paper is _____." Put that statement on an index card and prop it in front of you on your desk. Keep referring to it as you plan and write your essay.

In later stages of putting your paper together, revise your central statement until you have one sentence that summarizes your paper.

Here are some examples of central statements that evolved out of particular topics. Notice how the central statement relates to the original topic and to the title the writer chose.

Topic #1:   The Warsaw Ghetto

Central   The extermination of the Jews in Warsaw began when they

Statement: were gradually forced into progressively more crowded slum districts, then into a delineated ghetto, and finally into extermination camps.

Title: Ladder of Destruction: The Gradual Extermination of the Jews of Warsaw

Topic #2: Dance Notation

Central Statement: The method of dance notation developed by Rudolf Laban has transformed dance from an ephemeral art into an art that is as permanent as a musical score.

Title: Writing Dance: Rudolf Laban and Dance Notation

Notice that the central statement is neither a question nor a plan ("In this paper, I will cover. . . ."), but it does give you an idea of where the paper is going. Also notice how specific and pointed these central statements are—you know exactly what you are going to be reading about.

Discovering the Best Method of Organization for You

Most of us have been taught that the best way to organize is to make an outline and then follow it. This method is a sound one and works for writers who like to know ahead of time what they are going to say. However, many writers do not follow a pre-arranged outline and prefer instead to strike out and write before stopping to think about organization. You may be one of those. There is no one best way to organize, though some organizational strategies can point the way through the initial chaos.

There is, however, one method of organization which you should always *avoid*: Do not cover each of your sources one at a time.

The rest of this chapter presents four good ways to arrive at a well-organized essay.

Write First and Organize Later

With this method, you discover your organization through the process of writing. As you write, don't try to include all the facts from your notes. Don't worry about perfection. Just get down your ideas. Keep going *without starting over* until you reach the end.

When your ideas are all written, go back, read your notes, and decide which information will support each idea.

Write an abstract.   To test the organization of what you have written, try writing an abstract. An abstract is an overview of your paper—a summary of all the main points. It can provide you with an excellent way to check the effectiveness of your organization. If your paper is logically organized, your abstract will read like a smooth paragraph, one which could stand on its own.

Here are the steps in writing an abstract:

- Go through and write down—in list form—the key sentence in every major paragraph of your paper. Do not omit any main points.

- Read the sentences in sequence. Do they make sense? Does the abstract contain a complete idea? If you find gaps, important information has been left out. If so, add a key sentence and write a paragraph to go with it.

- Do the ideas follow logically? If not, rearrange your sentences and the respective paragraphs in the paper.

- Check to see if the sentences flow smoothly from one to the other. If not, add transitional phrases which will show the relationship between ideas. Then add the transitions to your paper. (For a sample abstract of a student paper, see "A Paper Using the APA Style" in the appendix.)

Write a Very Short First Draft

With this method, write the key assertions you want to prove—all in one paragraph. You should have between four and eight points that are generalizations—not specific facts.

Review your paragraph to make sure it flows smoothly and doesn't repeat the same idea two ways. Then take each of the sentences from your paragraph and make it the first sentence of a page. Go through your notes and decide which facts, quotations, and reasons will go under each sentence.

Now consider rearranging your paper—you may want to move one of the pages to make a better flow, combine two, or cut one.

Here's an example of a short draft (nine full sentences) of a paper by a student, Barney Yee, on the abuse of the Chinese in America from 1853 to 1904. As you read, think how each of these sentences could be expanded into a full paragraph.

Despite some of the harshest discrimination and violence faced by any immigrants to the United States, the Chinese have risen today to be considered a success story in the American melting pot. The anti-Chinese movement in America from 1850 to 1904 was characterized by anti-Chinese legislation, agitation by the popular press and politicians, and mob violence. The laws and ordinances directed against the Chinese took local, state, and federal forms. The popular press during that time portrayed the Chinese as sinister and devious, and labor parties were formed to protect white labor because Chinese were blamed for taking away jobs from whites. Eventually anti-Chinese hostility erupted into a series of brutal assaults. Chinese were driven from their homes, attacked by mobs, and brutalized by the police. The Chinese withdrew into their own enclaves until a second generation slowly emerged. Today most of the discrimination against Chinese-Americans has disappeared, and they have successfully assimilated into the mainstream of American life. But the young Chinese-Americans who have reaped the benefits of their forebears' sacrifices should never forget the great legacy they have been given.

Start with an Outline.

With this method, you make a map before you set out. Start with your central statement. Decide the key points that will demonstrate your main idea. One way to clarify these key points is to answer the following questions:

– How can I engage the reader in my subject?

– What does the reader need to know first?

- What are my strongest points?
- Out of all the possible conclusions, which do I want my reader to end up with?

The answers to these questions should tell you the main points of your paper.

Now survey your research notes for evidence that will support and clarify each main point. If you took notes on index cards, simply arrange the cards by topics.

From this rough plan, you can proceed to a working outline. Remember that you cannot include everything you learned without creating a chaotic paper. Instead, select the information that best demonstrates your key points.

In an outline, use the traditional system of numbers and letters to show which ideas are parts of other ideas and which facts support particular generalizations. Use *roman numerals* for the first level, *capital letters* for the second level, *arabic numerals* for the third level, and *lower case letters* for the fourth level. At any level you must have at least *two* items.

Here is a working outline of Barney Yee's full paper on the history of discrimination against Chinese-Americans. Notice that the writer

- uses phrases rather than whole sentences
- indicates facts and quotations
- includes the author and page where he found information
- includes his own ideas—especially at the end

A Litany of Abuse: The Chinese in America 1853–1904

I. Introduction—how easily we forget

   A. Refutation of Dr. Chiu—"not so bitter"

   B. Central statement: The Chinese have risen . . . U.S.

   C. A summary of my three main points

II. Anti-Chinese Legislation

   A. Local, state, and federal

B. List of laws

    1. 1853—Foreign Miners' License Tax Act

        a. quote Wu 11

        b. quote Tung 9

    2. 1855 People, Respondent, v. George Hall

        a. quote Wu 31, 12

        b. Open season on Chinese

    3. 1870—Sidewalk Ordinance (McCunn 73)

    4. 1882 Chinese Exclusion Act (Tung 18)

III. Agitation by Press and Politicians

A. Image of Chinese in Press

    1. Sinister, inscrutable, devious

    2. Threat to jobs

    3. Quote Tung 107—serving rats

B. Labor Agitation

    1. Drying up of gold market (McCunn 72)

    2. Workingmen's Party (McCunn 75)

C. Politicians

    1. Governor Stanford (Wu 106)

    2. Senator Jones (Wu 129)

IV. Mob Violence

A. Quote Gulick (qtd. in Lyman 15)

B. Instances of violence

1. 1852 Marysville, CA (Chen 137)

2. 1871 LA riots (Wu 152)

3. 1877 San Francisco (McCunn 78)

4. 1880 Denver (Tun 16)

5. 1885 Oregon (McCunn 81)

6. 1887 Many cities (McCunn 82)

C. Eastern examples

    1812 Boston (Wu 207)

D. No convictions—Chinese government protest (McCunn 81)

V. Gradual Improvement

A. Withdrawal into "enclaves" (Sowall 144)

B. 2nd Generation

    Legal rights—American-born (Swell 147)

C. The current generation

1. Not to forget

2. Not to deny links with predecessor

3. Refuting Dr. Chiu ("coolie")

4. Our hope to leave legacy to future Chinese-Americans

Turn your outline upside down.   You might have made a good outline and still not be satisfied with the organization of your paper. If so, open your mind to the possibility of a radical change of emphasis that makes your paper more exciting to you. Perhaps one part of your outline should become the whole paper and the other parts be dropped or subordinated. Perhaps you'd be better off to condense background information drastically. You might also see that you're covering the same information in two places and should cut one whole section.

Suppose that Barney Yee, in looking over his outline, feels the list of laws to be tedious. He might discover that his real interest is in the section on mob violence. In this case, he could make Part IV the main emphasis of his paper, move it to the front, expand it, and interweave Parts II (Anti-Chinese Legislation) and III (Agitation by Press and Politicians) with the central idea (Mob Violence). By making these changes, he has shifted the emphasis of his paper to the topic that most interests him.

Use a Formula

If you're having a tough time finding an organization for your topic, you may want to see if your material fits one of the following patterns:

- *Comparison*
- *Chronological Order*
- *Problem and Solution*
- *Cause and Effect*
- *Definition and Example*
- *Process*
- *Classification*

Even if you're not having a hard time with organization, your information may fit naturally into one of the above patterns of organization. The danger in using formulas is that they sometimes produce bland, boring papers. To work against monotony, keep clear in your mind what you want to emphasize and scale down whatever you can cover quickly.

Comparison

With this pattern, simply show how things are alike or different. Or use a combination of both to show how things are both alike and different. Keep your comparison within the field itself; going outside your subject field will mean double research for you. Possibilities for this formula are papers which present the pros and cons of an argument, or analyze contrasting theories, or compare two historical eras, major figures, or influences.

In organizing this paper, stick to one clear pattern. For example:

A — discuss fully

B — discuss fully

A/B — compare and/or contrast

Another possibility for organization is to take three or four ideas or specific statements and show how A and B fit in. Example:

Introduction — Introduce the ideas

Idea #1 ——— Illustrate with both A and B

Idea #2 ——— Illustrate with both A and B

In each pattern, continue until you've covered all the ideas.

Chronological Order

This pattern organizes material by time, moving either from the past forward to the present or from the hindsight of the present to the past. You must, however, select and subordinate details to give climactic interest; otherwise your paper will be monotonous. This pattern of development is useful for presenting biographical or historical studies, or for tracing a movement or trend. You can also use this pattern to describe your own growth in awareness as you conducted your research, if the assignment allows you to do so.

Problem and Solution

This pattern is well-suited to current topics (social issues, diseases, fitness, government policy) where you describe an on-going problem, analyze the various solutions that experts have proposed, and make your own judgment as to the best solution. For a more detailed discussion of this pattern, see chapter 18.

Cause and Effect

You can use this pattern to emphasize the causes that produce a particular result. For example, if you were explaining the effects of a single government regulation, you would start by explaining the regulation (the cause) and then discuss the various effects of the law. Or you can reverse the pattern and use Effect and Causes. In this case, if you were analyzing the causes of the decline in American inner cities, you would probably demonstrate the decline (the effect) in the first part of your paper and then enumerate the different causes of the decline.

Definition and Example

In this pattern, first present what you have learned about the meaning of a particular term or concept. Do not use the dictionary definition; instead, provide your own definition derived from your research. Then present examples that explain the meaning. This pattern is particularly good for case studies in psychology, medicine, law, or the arts. For example, you could define your understanding of the term *film noir* and then follow with studies of several representative films.

Process

This pattern breaks down your subject into steps of a process, telling how something is made or done. For example, you might do a paper which explains the procedure for converting a building from using fossil energy to using solar energy, or you might analyze the steps that led to the breakup of the Soviet Union. The challenge in writing a process paper is deciding how much detail is needed: If you tell too little, your reader can't follow you; if you tell too much, your reader gets bored or lost.

Classification

A classification pattern divides a topic into several divisions such as types, major parts, historical divisions, or groups. Some topics which lend themselves to this pattern are types of treatment for a disease, the subsidiaries of a corporation, the major battles of a war, or groups that make up a political movement.

Two Principles for Strong Organization

Weed Out Information You Don't Need

A good researcher collects a great quantity of information; a good writer selects the information which will demonstrate one important idea. Your paper must clarify the central statement that you have chosen and to do that you will have to omit distracting information. One of the most painful parts of the writing process is to *let go*: to admit that an interesting fact just does not contribute to the point you are stressing and will divert the reader from that point. Be ruthless. Don't include a fact or opinion or quotation or joke just because you like it. Every sentence must help to explain the point of the paragraph in which it is located; every paragraph must fall clearly into the logic of the whole paper.

Use Specific Information to Support General Assertions

A strong research paper—no matter how you go about writing it—will back up every general assertion with facts, examples, or logical reasons. After all, the purpose of research is to gather and interpret specific information. Early in your essay, you will need to assert your main general idea. After you make that main assertion, then you should present the parts of that main idea. Each will get a paragraph or several paragraphs. Within those paragraphs come the specifics: facts, reasons, examples, quotations, observable evidence. These details illuminate and justify your assertion. No paper is complete without this *specific* evidence.

In a Crunch

Especially in a crunch, you need a plan if you are to avoid disaster.

- Freewrite for at least twenty minutes to discover your main emphasis.

- Do not organize one source at a time. The plan must present your ideas, part by part—not simply one section from one source, one from another source, and so forth.

- Use one of the patterns explained on pages 75–77 of this chapter. Choose the one that best fits your emphasis. Make a rough outline of the parts of your paper.

- Make sure that you have evidence, examples, or arguments to back up each main point in your plan. You will need specific information in every paragraph.

- Don't try to include everything you have gathered. Stress two to four essential points. If you do this clearly and fully, your paper will be long enough.

Chapter 10

First Draft/Second Draft

No successful paper happens in a single draft. If you try to write your full paper in one draft, you put yourself under too much pressure to make everything perfect the first time around. To make the whole research paper more manageable, approach it in several stages, each time adding information and making adjustments.

Four Concerns You Can Defer Until Later

Right away you can put off worrying about four aspects of your paper:

The Perfect Introduction   Once you see how your paper comes out, you can go back and improve your introduction.

Spelling and Punctuation   Save this concern until the revision stage.

Documentation   You will add this information during your second or third draft.

Length   You don't have to aim for a certain length yet. When you have a full first draft on paper, you'll begin to see where information and explanations are needed.

Your First Draft

In your very first draft of the paper, you will need to get down your main ideas in order, explaining each one. It's important during this stage not to lose track of your own ideas that motivated you to go with this topic in the first place.

An excellent method for staying tuned in to your own ideas is to put all your notes and books into a closet and not refer to them until you've produced a complete first draft. This method forces you to pull together what you've found out and to write it in your own voice and style—rather than to be overly influenced by your notes. You will also be avoiding the worst kind of research paper, which is composed mostly of chunks taken from books and articles.

If at all possible, write your first full draft, all the way to your conclusion, in one sitting. Then give yourself a few hours or a day away from the work before you begin your next draft.

Keep in mind the following three ideas as you write your first draft: Your *central statement*, your *audience*, and your *writing voice*.

Start with a Central Statement

The simplest way to start is to look at the central statement you wrote while making a plan (see pp. 68–69). Keep it in front of you and, as you write your first draft, make sure that each part of your paper helps to support your central statement. As you write, you may find that a more important idea is taking over your paper. In this case, revise your central statement.

Aim Your Paper Right at Your Audience

Judge the expertise of your audience. Are you writing for the general reader or for an expert in the field? Usually, even when writing for a teacher, you cannot assume a lot of detailed knowledge. You will have to guide your reader. On the other hand, don't pad your paper with information that everybody knows. Anticipate your reader's questions and arguments. In general, put yourself in your reader's place.

Use a Strong Voice: Put "I" into Your Paper

A strong voice begins with "I." While some teachers may not allow you to use "I" in your papers, any time you have a choice, opt for doing so. This does not mean that you will fill your paper with "I think" and "in my opinion." These phrases are unnecessary and merely clutter up your paper.

A strong voice is also a confident one, so adopt a confident tone as you write. Remember that, through research, you have become somewhat of an authority on this subject. Write your paper from the position of this authority. State your case logically, objectively, and strongly. Use a straightforward style not very different from the style of other writing you have done: Don't fall into the trap of writing in a phony, artificial style just because this is a term paper.

Your Second Draft: Incorporating Information from Your Notes

You now have a straightforward statement of your main ideas but without many of the details. Your first draft may read very well, but it is not yet a research paper. The next step is to fill in the details from your research.

If Possible, Use a Computer

You may have written your first draft on a computer. If not, it would be a good idea to type it in now and store it for revision. The computer will allow you to *insert* quotations, facts, and documentation right into your first draft. Later it will allow you to move paragraphs and to make corrections without having to retype.

Reminders: Never turn off your machine without saving any changes and storing your updated work on a disc.

Don't erase deletions. Move them to the last page of your document for possible later use.

Search Your First Draft for Statements That Need Support

Now is the time to put in the facts, quotations, and fine points that you have gathered in your research. To decide what you need, look through your first draft for unsupported generalizations and unclear explanations. For instance, if you were to write, "Adoption of Korean children has become extremely expensive," this is a generalization, not a fact. To support your generalization, you would need to break down exactly how much the adoption costs and how that cost compares with other adoptions.

The second question to ask as you read each point is, "Have I told enough so that the reader can follow this point?" Look for places where you have used terms that may be unclear, where you need background information, or where you have omitted steps. For instance, suppose that in a paper on world hunger you assert that if Americans were to give up eating meat, we could feed the hungry people of the world. This statement is not comprehensible unless you explain that we feed our grain to animals that we then eat, instead of using the grain to feed people. To make your assertion clear, you need not only statistics, but a logical explanation of the place of grain and meat in the food chain.

In short, look for points that your reader might doubt or might not understand.

Raid Your Notes for Facts and Quotations

Once you see the places where evidence and explanation are needed, you can retrieve your notes from the closet. Reread them and select the facts, quotations, and other information that you need to support the various parts of your paper. Make a note on your first draft of where each piece of information will go. As you review your notes, don't get pulled off course by material that seems interesting or significant but that doesn't fit clearly into one of your paragraphs.

Now you have lined up the places where you need details and the details that will go into each place. Next you can weave these details gracefully into your paper.

For more specific advice for drafting papers on literature, see chapter 17; for advice on drafting papers on social issues, see chapter 18.

In a Crunch

If you find that you are stuck in generating your first draft, here are a few ways to break the spell.

Talk to a classmate or friend.   A brief exchange about your topic with someone else can often get your juices flowing. Immediately after the conversation, write down your thoughts and responses.

Do half an hour of reading.   For thirty minutes (by the clock), read one new source about your topic. A new slant may get you going.

Respond to this question: What matters to me most about this subject? Put this question at the top of a page and answer it as fully as possible. Every time you start to wind down, return to the question and re-ask it to yourself.

Freewrite.   Set a timer or clock for *three* minutes. On a separate sheet of paper, write about your topic for three minutes only. At the end of the three minutes, write a sentence summarizing what you wrote. You can repeat this exercise as many times as you like, but keep the three-minute limit each time.

Take a break.   Give yourself some fallow time by going for a walk, napping, or getting a bite to eat. Or just take a few minutes to sit and close your eyes and visualize some aspect of your topic. Afterwards, open your eyes and write down what you saw. Your unconscious mind may well use this break time to move you further along in your project.

Chapter
11

Varying the Way You Use
Your Sources

Most of what we have been discussing in Part III are general ways in which you can make any paper you write stronger and more dynamic. However, a major distinction between other papers and a research paper is that in a research paper you have to refer to the sources of your information in order to validate the claims you are making.

A good research paper is not just a compilation of information from books, articles, and other sources. You must always stress your perspective, your sequence of ideas. You are your reader's guide through this topic. So your voice, not the voices of your sources, must control the paper, especially in the introduction, the beginnings and ends of paragraphs, and in the conclusion.

One big challenge in writing a paper based on research is incorporating your source material into your essay in an inviting way. Nothing is duller than a dull research paper. Here are two general guidelines to help you write a documented paper which reads more like a persuasive, interesting essay than a required research paper.

- Weave the expert's name into the text of your paper. This creates an authoritative tone in your paper while also giving credit to your sources in a graceful way.

- Alternate between using direct quotation, paraphrase, and summary. Use all three of these in a balanced way throughout your paper.

As you insert information from your sources into your paper, you also need to tell where the information came from. For the correct method of documentation, see chapter 14. You will notice that in our examples in this chapter we have included parenthetical citations of our sources—the method explained in chapter 14. Further, we follow each quotation with its bibliographical citation.

The following section gives you specific guidelines for using *direct quotation, paraphrase,* and *summary.*

Direct Quotations

Direct quotations can be

- Another person's written words
- Another person's spoken words—whether from radio, television, or personal interview

When you use direct quotation, use the *exact* wording from your material and frame the words with quotation marks.

As Doreen Kimura explains, "The effects of sex hormones on brain organization occur so early in life that from the start the environment is acting on differently wired brains in girls and boys" (119).

Kimura, Doreen. "Sex Differences in the Brain." Scientific American. Sept. 1992: 118–25.

Even if you use only a phrase or a key word, you must indicate that it has been taken from someone else by placing it within quotation marks.

Evidence shows that the brains of boys and girls are "differently wired" (Kimura 119).

Use direct quotations to:

- Repeat word for word a statement that merits repetition
- Report technical or unusual information that cannot be paraphrased
- Present precisely what someone has said so that you can comment on it
- Capture the style of someone's speech
- Give a particularly authoritative ring to what you're explaining

Use Direct Quotations Effectively

Be Sure that Your Own Ideas Control the Paper   Don't let your sources' words dominate your paper. Most of the words and ideas in the paper should be your own; use the words and opinions of others only to support the points you are making. Never try to use every quotation you've taken down. Quotations should make up no more than fifteen percent of your paper.

Keep the Quotations Short   It's tempting to use big blocks of information, especially when the information is well written. Resist this temptation. You can quote complete sentences at times—sometimes even two sentences, but seldom more. A better choice is to incorporate fragments of direct quotations into your *own* sentences.

> Medical treatment of racehorses has changed in recent years, becoming "misdirected from the art of healing to the craft of portfolio management" (Ferraro 8).
>
> Ferraro, Gregory. "The Corruption of Nobility: Rise and Fall of Thoroughbred Racing in America." The North American Review May–June 1992: 4–8.

Comment on Each Quotation   State your point clearly before you use a quotation and, after you've quoted it, make a comment about it. Ask yourself, "What's the point of this quotation?" Make that point clear to your reader.

> East Africa is increasingly plagued by mass hunger which continues to be fired by overpopulation, crop failure, and wars. Jonathan Stevenson says, "There are no meccas in East Africa, only shifting places of refuge for starving and uprooted people" (16), and these conditions don't appear likely to change in the near future.
>
> Stevenson, Jonathan. "Food for Naught." The New Republic 21 Sept. 1992: 13–14, 16.

In general, do not begin or end a paragraph with a direct quotation. Start and end each paragraph with your own words.

Clearly Identify Each Quotation   Use identifying tags for each quotation. Never leave quotations dangling in your paper. Always make clear who is speaking and in what context, usually by leading into the quotation.

According to Marion Levine, ". . . ."

She says, ". . . ."

E. M. Forster believes that ". . . ."

He explains that ". . . ."

Weave Your Sources Together   Don't quote from your sources one by one. Don't have a block of quotations from one source in a part of your paper and then all the quotations from another one somewhere else. Instead, weave the quotations together. Note how Chris McDonnell, a student, juxtaposes quotations against each other:

> In various parts of the world, fish hatcheries are allowing some of their fish to escape and to spread disease to wild fish. Laurie MacBride describes "new parasites and diseases" (26) occurring in the Georgia Bay of Ontario. Stephen Cline describes a similar problem "traced to a hatchery" (36) in Norway. The problem is further aggravated, as Marcia Barinaga points out, because antibiotics used in hatcheries eventually "promote the growth of antibiotic-resistant bacteria" in the ocean (630).

> Barinaga, Marcia. "Fish, Money, and Science in Puget Sound." News and Comment. 9 Feb. 1990: 631.
> Cline, Stephen. "Down on the Fish Farm." Sierra Mar.–Apr. 1989: 34–38.
> MacBride, Laurie. "Alliance Fights for Georgia Strait." Canadian Dimension Oct. 1990: 24–27.

Incorporate Quotations into Complete Sentences   Make certain that you incorporate your quotations into clear and complete sentences that make sense. You can also use your own running commentary to link several short quotations.

> The music that Frederick Douglass found so personally moving also touched W. E. B. DuBois, who devoted a chapter of *The Souls of Black Folk* to African-American folk songs. DuBois considered these songs "the greatest gift of the Negro people" to American culture; in fact, he claims that they are "the most beautiful expression of human experience born this side [of] the seas" (182).

> DuBois, W. E. B. *The Souls of Black Folk*. New York: Washington Square, 1970.

Copy the Quotation Exactly   Retain the writer's spelling and punctuation. Double check to make sure you have not left out anything.

Punctuate Direct Quotations Correctly

Use Quotation Marks for a Few Words   For quotations of one word or a few words, simply incorporate the word or phrase into your sentence and then enclose the word or words in double quotation marks. Use no other punctuation.

> William Irvine considers Thomas Huxley's view of religion to be "negative" (404).

> Irvine, William. Apes, Angels & Victorians. New York: Time, 1963.

Use a Comma to Separate a Quotation from a Tag   Use a comma *after* a tag when it introduces a quotation. Use a comma *after* a quotation when a tag follows it.

> Sharon Mazer says, "Professional wrestling is frequently criticized as a crude, brutal sport that lacks even the honesty of competition" (97).

> "Professional wrestling is frequently criticized as a crude, brutal sport that lacks even the honesty of competition," says Sharon Mazer (97).

However, use *no* comma when you use *that*:

> Sharon Mazer says that "professional wrestling is frequently criticized as a crude, brutal sport that lacks even the honesty of competition." (97).

> Mazer, Sharon. "The Doggie Doggie World of Professional Wrestling." The Drama Review 34 (Winter 1990): 96–122.

Use a Colon to Set Off Quotations of One or Two Sentences   A colon is an effective way to set off a rather long quotation of one or two sentences, or as a way to make a quotation stand out. Usually you make a full statement before the colon, and the quotation illustrates that statement. Do not use tags such as "he says" when you use a colon.

> Ron Matou describes the universal symbolism of mountain-climbing: "Mountaineering is one of the ways in which the human spirit has aspired to transcend its physical limitations" (10).

> Matou, Ron. "Quest for the Summit." Parabola Winter 1992: 10–15.

Place Periods and Commas Inside the Closing Quotation Marks

> The Bible advises us to "turn the other cheek." When Greta Garbo said "I want to be alone," she really meant it.

Place Semicolons Outside the Closing Quotation Marks

> William J. Doherty concluded that most Americans "believe that the stable, two-parent family is the best environment for raising children"; however, he also found that this environment is far from typical in contemporary America (35).

> Doherty, William J. "Private Lives, Public Values." Psychology Today May–June 1992: 32–37, 82.

Place Most Question Marks and Exclamation Points Inside

"What did he know and when did he know it?" was the most quoted line from the hearings.

However, if *you* are asking or exclaiming, the mark goes *outside*:

What did Joyce Cary mean when he wrote that genius is "much more fragile than talent"? (51).

Cary, Joyce. Art and Reality: Ways of the Creative Process. New York: Harper, 1958.

Indent Long Quotations Quotations of *three or more lines* must be set off by indenting each line ten spaces from the left margin. Do not use quotation marks.

Stephen Nachmanovitch, in his book *Free Play*, says that improvisation is not something that happens just in the arts, but also in everyday life:

We are all improvisers. The most common form of improvisation is ordinary speech. As we talk and listen, we are drawing on a set of building blocks (vocabulary) and rules for combining them (grammar). These have been given to us by our culture. But the sentences we make with them may never have been said before and may never be said again. Every conversation is a form of jazz. (17)

Nachmanovitch, Stephen. *Free Play: The Power of Improvisation in Life and the Arts*. Los Angeles: Tarcher, 1990.

After the quotation, return to the left margin and discuss what was important in the quotation. However, you should rarely use long quotations. Save them for unusual statements that really deliver a punch.

Use Ellipsis to Indicate Words Left Out Often you want to quote only part of a statement. Perhaps the middle is irrelevant to your point or you want to omit unnecessary words. Use ellipsis marks, three periods separated by spaces, to indicate you have left out material; use four periods when the omitted material itself contains a period:

In assessing pre-Columbian agriculture, Brian Fagan concludes that "Native Americans domesticated a truly astounding range of plants. . . . They were among the most expert of farmers in the world of 1492" (34).

Fagan, Brian. "If Columbus Had Not Called." History Today May 1992: 30–36.

Use Brackets to Indicate That a Word Has Been Changed or Added

Sometimes a quotation taken out of context is not completely clear and you need to change or explain a word. If so, place your words in *brackets*.

> An article in *Popular Mechanics* tells how "the FSX [Future Shock Experimental—a new bicycle] also has cable-activated hydraulic disc brakes similar to those used on motorcycles" (100).

> "Bike to the Future." Popular Mechanics Aug. 1992: 100–01.

Use Single Quotation Marks for a Quotation within a Quotation

When you quote someone who is quoting someone else, you then have a quotation within a quotation. Simply use single quotation marks (the apostrophe mark) for the second speaker.

> Jerome Bruner points out that narrative "must be concrete: it must 'ascend to the particular,' as Karl Marx put it" (60).

> Bruner, Jerome. Acts of Meaning. Cambridge: Harvard UP, 1990.

Use *Sic* to Indicate an Error That Belongs to Your Source, Not to You

If there is a mistake in a quotation you need to use, reprint the error exactly, but right after it add *sic* (in brackets), which means that you have reproduced the error as you found it.

> Analyzing the art of quilting, Patricia Mainardi says that "Time seems to be the principle [sic] ingredient in traditional quilts" (52).

> Mainardi, Patricia. "Quilt Survivals and Revivals." Arts Magazine May 1988: 49–57.

Paraphrase

When you *paraphrase*, you take someone else's words and put them into your own words. That means you *reword* a statement completely and restate another person's ideas. If you can paraphrase an idea, then you know you have grasped it. The challenge in paraphrasing is to capture the exact sense of a passage or statement without using the same words: You put the information into your own words; it should sound like you. Most of the notes you take while doing research should be paraphrased and, therefore, much of your final paper will automatically be in paraphrase.

Don't forget: Paraphrased material must be documented the same as direct quotation. You must acknowledge your source of information.

Use paraphrase to:

- write in your own voice and style instead of over-quoting
- use information that is not necessarily written in an interesting or concise manner
- bring technical information down to an easy reading level
- clarify a point—that is, write a paraphrase that is clearer than the original
- report a series of facts

Use Paraphrase Correctly:

Write Your Paraphrase from Memory   Without consulting your notes, write your paraphrase using your own words; then go back and check for accuracy. This method will keep you from plagiarizing as well as help you see if you understand what you've read.

Do Not Copy Any Words Directly from Your Source   If you need to consult your source while writing from memory, play it safe and avoid borrowing exact words. Make a conscious effort to restate everything in your own words. If you incorporate any wording from your source, you are employing *direct quotation* with the paraphrase, so use quotation marks around those words.

Check the Definitions of Any Unusual Words   Look up any unusual words in the dictionary to be certain that you completely understand the passage word for word.

Make Certain that Your Paraphrase Can Stand Alone   Your paraphrase should be readable and clear all on its own and should not depend upon reference to your source for clarification.

Identify Your Source within the Paraphrase   As a general rule, you should identify your source by name and area of expertise; include your own judgment of how the source has presented an idea—in other words, provide a slight interpretation.

Sample Paraphrases for Study

Here are two short paraphrases that will give you some ideas for how a paraphrase should be constructed:

Original

When a woman is admitted to higher education—particularly graduate school—it is often made to sound as if she enters a sexually neutral world of "disinterested" and "universal" perspectives. It is assumed that coeducation means the equal education, side by side, of women and men. Nothing could be further from the truth. . . . (134)

Rich, Adrienne. "Toward a Woman-Centered University." On Lies, Secrets and Silence. New York: Norton, 1979.

Paraphrase

When women enter graduate school, they harbor the illusion that they are becoming part of a world which will provide them with an education equal to what men get. Not so, warns Adrienne Rich (134).

Original

Every so often out of the millions of the human population, a six-year-old child or a teen-age youth dies of old age. The cause of this curious disease, known as progeria, or premature aging, is totally unknown. (108)

Eiseley, Loren. The Immense Journey. New York: Vintage, 1957.

Paraphrase

Anthropologist Loren Eiseley reports that premature aging, a strange disease with no known causes, sometimes kills very young people (108).

Summary

Like *paraphrase*, a *summary* restates someone else's words. When you summarize, you restate an idea in considerably shorter form—*sum it up*—in your own words. You can summarize anything from a paragraph to a complete book. You will use *direct quotation* and *paraphrase* far more often than *summary* in writing your research papers. However, summary is an excellent way to add related or contrasting ideas to your paper without getting off track. You can bring entire books into your paper with only a sentence or two and thereby provide even more authority for your position.

Don't forget: Summarized material, just like direct quotations and paraphrases, must be documented. You must acknowledge your source of information.

Use Summary to:

- Acknowledge a conflicting idea

- Introduce a related idea without too much detail

- Cover a large amount of material in a few words

Use Summary Effectively:

Read the Material Carefully   Be certain that you understand each idea and how each idea is related to the other. Look up the definition of any words you are not completely sure of.

Choose Only What Is Essential   Carefully ferret out only the major ideas. Delete extraneous material such as examples, entertaining passages, or rhetorical statements.

Summarize Sequentially   Take down the ideas in the order in which they were written. When you present the ideas, you may sometimes want to rearrange the points for greater emphasis, but it is usually better to summarize in the author's sequence of ideas.

Stick Closely to the Text   Condense only the ideas you have read. Do not add anything new. A summary is not the place to add your own interpretations.

As with paraphrase, summary requires that you use your own words. Also, it's a good idea to identify your source within the summary, just as you do with paraphrase.

Sample Summaries for Study:

Original

Paradox has characterized the development of the short story in the United States. Although it is the only major literary form of essentially American origin and the only one in which American writers have from the beginning tended to excel, for decades it was considered a subliterary genre, which until relatively recent times most critics refused to consider as important as the more traditional forms of poetry, drama, and the novel. (1)

Peden, William. The American Short Story: Continuity and Change 1940–1975. 2nd ed. Boston: Houghton, 1975.

Summary

According to William Peden, the short story, the only literary form that originated in America, was once considered by critics to be inferior to poetry, drama, and the novel (1).

Original

A demonstrably false series of assumptions keeps a great many writers from seriously considering self-publishing, which is a shame because many of them could earn more money and have more fun if they brought out their own work. Constructed with one part ignorance, one part laziness and one part unadulterated snobbery, the chain of thought might be summarized as follows: I am a writer; a writer's job is to express ideas, images and information in words; after a writer has done this job, noncreative types should pronounce it good and take it over, leaving the writer free to write some more. (153)

Appelbaum, Judith. How to Get Happily Published. 4th ed. New York: Harper, 1992.

Summary   Judith Appelbaum advises that publishing their own work is a way for writers to get themselves in print *and* make more money. But many writers feel self-publishing is beneath them or that it is not part of their job (153).

A summary of Appelbaum's entire book might go like this: Judith Appelbaum's book *How to Get Happily Published* is based on the premise that getting published is something writers can learn about—and accomplish. She provides a map for doing so, from getting words on paper to getting a foot in the door.

A final reminder: Use all three methods—*direct quotation, paraphrase,* and *summary*—for incorporating your sources rather than jamming your paper with too many quotations. In any case, the ideas from your sources must be subordinated to the points that you are stressing. Ultimately, *you* are the authority behind your paper.

A Checklist for Revision

Large-Scale Revision

☐ Organization—Outline what you have written

☐ Completeness—Compare your original outline

☐ Clarity—Search for unclear terms, quotations, facts, points

☐ Introduction & Conclusion & Title—Make sure they fit the paper

Small-Scale Revision

☐ Accuracy of names and numbers

☐ Accuracy of quotations

☐ Accuracy of documentation

☐ Style—balance of formal and informal

☐ Transitions between ideas

☐ Transitions into and out of facts and quotations

☐ Spelling—including small words, such as "to" and "too"

☐ Periods—no run-on sentences or sentence fragments

☐ Agreement—singular and plural, especially in introduction and conclusion

☐ Verb tenses—consistency

☐ Punctuation with quotations

☐ Titles—underlined or quoted

Final Manuscript Preparation

☐ Format: typeface and spacing

☐ Long quotations—set off, without quotation marks

☐ Illustrations—legibility and sufficient space

☐ Coversheet and page numbers

☐ Assembly of paper with all its parts

☐ Examination of printed copy: printer errors

☐ Proofreading of final copy

Chapter 12

Producing a Finished Paper

The most tempting—and absolutely the most dangerous—place to slack off is at the moment that you have a full draft of your research paper. It is always a relief to be at this stage, and for most people it occurs very close to the deadline for submission. However, your paper is not finished until you've revised it. Revision is your opportunity to turn an average research project into a superlative presentation.

There are two kinds of revision: *large-scale* and *small-scale*. First you need to look at the overall content of your paper. Later you will concern yourself with the details.

The last step is to put your *final manuscript* into proper form.

Large-Scale Revision

Large-scale revision means taking a look at the major parts of your paper to see if they work smoothly together. It's foolish at this stage to fine-tune details which eventually might get cut out of your paper. Instead you'll need to go through the paper methodically revising for three aspects: *organization*, *completeness*, and *clarity*. Finally, you will return to your *introduction and conclusion* to make sure that they fit your actual paper. And you will settle on a *title*.

Organization

A good way to check your organization is to write an outline of the actual paper that you have written. Write down a phrase to represent each paragraph of the paper.

Look at the sequence of your points. Are related points together? Is the sequence logical? Rearrange or cut any that seem out of place. Then make the corresponding changes in your paper.

Is anything unrelated? Sometimes the source material was so interesting that you felt you *had* to include it. Now you notice that it does not develop your main point at all. Be ruthless in deleting unrelated material.

Check your paragraphing. Do some long paragraphs need to be divided? Are some paragraphs too short? Can they be combined? Do they proceed logically from one to the other?

Completeness

The outline you made of the paper as you have written it is a good tool for making sure that your paper is complete.

Is anything missing? Check the outline for gaps. If so, add appropriate material.

If you wrote an outline when you were planning your paper, check that original outline against the outline you have just written and reorganize or fill in gaps as necessary.

Review your notes to see if you have omitted any information you had planned to use in a particular place. If so, add it into your paper. However, be careful not to lose the sense of the whole paper at this stage—don't stick in all sorts of extra information just because you have it.

Clarity

Make sure that you have been clear. Will your reader be able to follow your line of thought and understand each individual point?

Here are some points that might not be clear:

Terms   You might need to explain or define some terms.

Quotations   The reader needs to know who said them and how each one fits the point you are making.

Facts   Make clear how the fact fits in with what you are saying.

Complex Points   Have you taken the reader with you step by step?

Have you featured the most important facts? Be careful not to bury the most significant point in the middle of a paragraph or series. Note that the middle is the weakest position in any list; the final position is the strongest.

Ask yourself what the reason is for including each fact. Although you won't actually write, "I have included this fact because . . . ," your paper should make that reason clear. After each fact, add your comments to explain or interpret the information.

Introduction and Conclusion

Now is the time to take a second look at your introduction and conclusion. Think about what your paper says, and make sure the introduction points the way. Your central statement should stand out at the beginning or the end of your introductory paragraph—or paragraphs. Your conclusion should do more than just repeat your main points: It should leave the reader with a final emphasis, the point you most want to stress.

Write both the introduction and conclusion with energy and force. You might even write a few alternatives to see which one feels right. You don't want to slide into your paper at the start or to limp out of it at the end.

Title

Your title is an announcement of the content of your paper. Therefore, it has to be specific so the reader knows the paper's subject. If your title is too broad, it will be misleading—your reader would expect a book. Instead of a broad title such as "Nursing Homes," use a more specific title such as "The Rising Cost of Nursing Homes in Oklahoma."

Your title is also an advertisement for your paper; it says, "Read me." Therefore, your title should have punch. A title like "Family Stress" can easily be turned into something catchier, such as "Stress—It's All in the Family."

You can give your paper two titles. It is common to do so, putting a colon between them. One half can be poetic, the other half can be informative.

> Killing Dolphins: As Easy as Opening a Can of Tuna
> The Voice of the Land: The Prairie in Willa Cather's My Antonia

Remember not to use quotation marks or underlining for your own title.

Small-Scale Revision

Small-scale revision means looking closely at the details of your paper: checking the *accuracy* of information, the *style* of your writing, the smoothness of your *transitions*, and *grammar and usage*.

Accuracy

You want to be sure that you catch any mistakes in the details of your paper. Here are the most important places to look:

Numbers   Make sure any use of a number is accurate.

Names   Make sure that all names are correctly spelled.

Quotations   Make sure every quotation is a word-for-word reproduction of the original. Do you have quotation marks around all wording taken directly from your sources?

Citations   Make sure that the author and page number are accurate for all citations. You can highlight citations with a highlighter pen so that they stand out from the rest of the paper. That way you can more easily see and correct them.

Remember whether the information from a source is in your words (needing no quotation marks) or someone else's (and therefore framed by quotation marks), you must have a citation (see chapter 14).

Style

An essential step to check the style of your paper is to read it out loud. As you read aloud, listen for places that seem either too wordy and formal or too informal. On the one hand, you want to be *clear*—using plain English as much as possible instead of technical jargon. You don't want to pad your paper with wordy phrases, such as "due to the fact that." On the other hand, you should not have cute little remarks to the reader ("Ha! Ha!") or refer to authors on a first-name basis ("Ben says . . . ") or constantly be apologizing for your own opinion with phrases such as "I think" or "in my opinion." Above all, make sure you have put information into your own style of writing rather than heavily quoting or merely changing a few words from your sources.

Transitions

The flow of your paper depends upon your providing a smooth transition from one sentence to the next, from one paragraph to the next, and from one idea to the next. Transitions provide the bridges which carry your reader through the different segments of your paper. Check to see if your paper moves smoothly from one part to the other. If not, go back and add transitional words and phrases that will show the relationship between your sentences, paragraphs, and ideas. For example, at the beginning of each paragraph, make clear how it builds on the previous paragraph, and how the two major ideas are connected.

A special type of transition particular to research papers—*directive expressions*—link your ideas to the quotations and facts from your sources. Here are some examples of transition words and directive expressions that you might find useful:

Transition Phrases	Directive Expressions
However	According to . . .
Nevertheless	_____ points out that . . .
For example	As _____ has stated . . .
On the other hand	(or said, concluded,
In any case	observed, discovered)
Despite the evidence	

Grammar and Usage

This is the point at which to check and double-check punctuation, spelling, and any aspect of grammar and usage that gives you trouble. Use a dictionary and a handbook. Make sure that you never guess; look up any rule that you are not sure of.

- Check the spelling of words that are often confused such as *to* and *too*, *then* and *than*. A computer spell-check will miss this type of error.

- Check the placement of periods to avoid run-on sentences and sentence fragments.

- Check agreement (singulars and plurals) of subjects and verbs, pronouns and antecedents.

- Check verb tenses to be sure you have not shifted back and forth between present and past.

- Check to see that commas and other punctuation used with quotations are correct (see pp. 85–90).

- Check that titles of books, periodicals and other long works are underlined or italicized and that titles of articles, chapters, and other short works are enclosed in quotation marks.

Final Manuscript Preparation

In the actual preparation of your manuscript, check the following points:

Format

Paper   Type on plain white 8½ x 11 typing paper. Do not use onion skin or erasable bond. Separate the pages and remove the perforated edges from computer paper.

Typeface   If you use a computer, use a standard size type face (not italics, all capitals, or large print).

Vertical Space   Double-space the entire paper, including the *Works Cited* page as well as any long quotations which have been set off.

Margins   Use margins of 1–1½ inches on all four sides. Do not justify (line up) the right margin.

Paragraphing   Indent the first line of each paragraph five spaces. Or use block format (no indentation of the first line) and add an extra return between paragraphs. Do not mix these two formats.

Spacing with Periods and Commas

- Two spaces after periods and colons

- One space after commas and semicolons

- No spaces before periods, commas, hyphens, or dashes

Word Division   Either avoid dividing words at the end of a line or divide between syllables.

Page Endings   Be sure that you leave sufficient bottom margin. Do not end the page with only half a line of type unless you are at the end of a paragraph. Instead, continue to the right margin, even if you have to end the page in mid-sentence.

Long Quotations   Set off long quotations (those taking three lines or more) by indenting every line 10 spaces on the left. Don't indent from the right.

Headings   In a short paper, headings may seem disruptive and make the paper choppy. If you decide, for a longer paper, that headings are important, limit yourself to one level of heading: centered or aligned with the left margin and typed in capitals and lowercase. You can make headings stand out by underlining or boldfacing them—or you can use a contrasting typeface.

Illustrations   If you plan to insert graphics or illustrations into the body of your paper, be sure to leave space for them as you type. Otherwise, place graphics at the end of the paper (after the *Works Cited*) and label that section "Appendix." For detailed instructions on the use of illustrations, see chapter 20.

Pagination   Number each page after the first. You should also put your last name in the upper righthand corner of every page after the first.

Coversheet Prepare a coversheet which includes

- the title, centered vertically and horizontally

- your name, the course, the professor's name and the date in the bottom righthand corner

Assembling the Paper

Once your paper is typed, there is a conventional order for assembling it:

- Coversheet

- Abstract (if required)

- Outline, including thesis statement (if required)

- The paper (do not repeat the title on page one)

- *Works Cited* page

- Appendix (if you have one)

- Supplementary Bibliography (an optional list of sources you read but did not cite)

Staple your paper *once* in the upper lefthand corner. See "A Paper Using the APA Style" in the appendix for a fully assembled paper.

Proofreading and Eliminating Keyboarding Errors

After your paper is printed, proofread your manuscript several times. Make neat corrections with ink or correction fluid.

Typographical errors and computer glitches, even though they don't show a lack of knowledge on your part, do show a lack of care. Find them and fix them. To guard against them:

- Use the spell-check if you type on a computer.

- Proofread for errors the spell-check won't catch, such as *it's* for *its* and *there* for *their*. Read each page one word at a time on the screen or in the typewriter.

- Proofread your documentation for spacing and punctuation. (See chapters 14–16.)

- Make sure that every quotation mark and parenthesis has a partner.

- Make sure that the deletions you made got deleted, that the insertions got inserted, and that the adjacent letters and spaces did not get messed up in the process.

- Correct all printer errors. Even though the machine made the mistake, you're responsible for fixing it.

In a Crunch

If you have only a few hours left until deadline and still have a mess on your hands, here are a few ways you might pull through:

- Enlist a friend's help. Have him or her read over your paper and make suggestions.

- If your paper is typed but not on a word processor, use scissors and tape to rearrange the parts or to cut out excess material. Photocopy the reassembled paper if there is no time to retype.

- If you need to insert material, either type or handwrite it on a separate page, labeling it, for example, "insert page 7A." In your manuscript, indicate with an asterisk or the word "insert" where the insert should go.

- No matter how pressed you are, do not submit a paper that you have not proofread at least once or twice. Even at the last minute, make neat corrections with a black pen. Use correction fluid or tape if you have to.

- If you don't have an acceptable paper by the deadline, take what you have completed to show the teacher when you request an extension. Even teachers who don't ordinarily accept late papers might be convinced—upon seeing a partial manuscript—to grant a few hours' reprieve.

Here is a sample page from a student paper illustrating correct format and MLA Citation Style. (The complete paper can be found in the appendix, pp. 189–194.)

Pesiri 4

strong, and independent woman. As Alison Lurie says of fairy

tales in general:

> These stories suggest a society in which women are
>
> as competent and active as men . . . Gretel, not
>
> Hansel, defeats the witch. (42)

Bettelheim makes similar observations about the importance of

Gretel's transformation. After the examples of the evil step-

mother and the witch, it is "important to see that a female can

be a rescuer as well as a destroyer" (164). He cites the exam-

ple of a woman who loved "Hansel and Gretel" since she was a

child. As an adult she realized why she loved the story so much:

it had helped her to settle an uneasy relationship with her

brother. She was very dependent on her older brother as they

were growing up and resented it (16–17).

The children find valuable treasure hidden in the witch's

house and gather it up. Hansel and Gretel have gained self-

Part Four

Giving Credit to Your Sources: Documentation

Chapter 13

Plagiarism: Theft of Other People's Ideas

Research papers are routinely assigned in college because they provide a fast means of self-education. If you research correctly, you really can become an authority in your field of study. However, you have to give credit to your sources of information—for their facts, their ideas, and their phrasing. You are, after all, building on what others have discovered and adding your voice to the general conversation on the subject. You are sharing with your readers both what others have reported and your own interpretation and emphasis.

Plagiarism occurs when you *present other people's facts, ideas, or words as if they were your own—whether you do so deliberately, carelessly, or unconsciously.*

The difficulty in reporting research is retaining your own voice and point of view while presenting the information and ideas of others.

Deliberate Plagiarism, Careless Plagiarism, and Unconscious Plagiarism

Deliberate Plagiarism

Deliberate plagiarism happens when you copy from books and other sources—either word-for-word or with some changes—with the purpose of presenting this material as your own writing. If you hand in a paper that contains someone else's phrasing or ideas without giving credit to that person, you are taking big risks:

If your teacher proves that you have plagiarized, you might fail the course or you might be permanently expelled from the college or university. These punishments have been upheld in court.

If your teacher even suspects that you have plagiarized, your course grade may well suffer.

You can save yourself a lot of trouble if you assiduously avoid plagiarism:

- Do not use someone else's phrasing without quotation marks.
- Do not use someone else's idea without telling specifically where you found that idea.
- Do not collaborate with a friend to the extent that your friend dictates the ideas or phrasing of your paper.
- Do not hand in a paper that you have written for another course without your teacher's consent. Some teachers consider this to be another form of plagiarism.

Careless Plagiarism

Careless plagiarism happens when you take notes carelessly and therefore don't know when the ideas and phrasing are yours or someone else's. It is very tempting to copy down information exactly as written in a source, particularly when time is a factor. Later you may forget what in the notes was copied (and thus must be quoted) and what was paraphrased. However, *in both cases* the material must be credited to the person who originated it, and failure to do so is plagiarism.

Be aware of how easy it is for a teacher to spot plagiarism in a student paper, and how seriously most teachers regard such a transgression. First, your teacher is probably already familiar with your style, but even in a large class where the teacher gets few papers from each student, the teacher will recognize the style of professional sources in the field and may even be extremely familiar with the sources you have used.

Unconscious Plagiarism

Unconscious plagiarism happens when, after immersing yourself in specialized material, you retain the style of the sources—rather like what can happen when you visit a strongly accented region of the country for several months. In the same way, you may also inadvertently adopt whole phrases or technical terms that you never used before. Each discipline has its own vocabulary, and some of that diction will work itself into your writing. Part of this effect, which is positive, is learning to think and speak like an anthropologist, psychologist, historian, music critic, or expert in whatever the field; the negative effect is the risk of plagiarism if you use another person's distinctive phrase without quotation marks.

Preventing Plagiarism

Here are seven steps you can take both to prevent plagiarism and to assure a well-written paper:

Take notes carefully.   Most of the time, put what you read into your own words—being careful to put quotation marks around any exact wording from your source. If you don't have time to take notes, make a photocopy of the relevant pages. Be sure to write on the photocopy all bibliographical information, including page number.

Always know where your information came from.   Don't count on your memory. When you hear a relevant announcement on the radio, for example, immediately jot down the time, day, and station. Or if you are skimming an article that has only one usable fact, write all the bibliographic information down anyway. You'll be surprised how often such bits of information insist on being used and how hard they are to track down later.

Think as you take notes.   Don't just automatically take down what you find. Whenever possible, condense your note to its essential point, or write a note to yourself (labeled ''my idea'') that makes a connection to another source's idea or to another point that this source is making.

Write your first draft without consulting notes or books.   Your ideas must begin your essay, govern your essay, and end your essay. Only after you've written out your ideas in order can you decide which facts and quotations you need to back them up. To avoid careless plagiarism, write your first draft with your notes and books out of the room.

Don't throw anything away.   As you're copying material from your notes into your paper, keep a folder or box handy to store everything until you've completed the project. That way, if you need to verify a statistic or a page number, you can still do so without having to go back to the library.

Master the techniques of direct quotation, paraphrase and summary.
These are the three methods by which you incorporate what you have learned from your research. Study chapter 11, ''Varying the Way you Use your Sources.''

Be conscious of your sources as you put your paper together. (See Chapter 14 or 16.)   When revising your paper, place citations immediately into the line after you have used material from your sources. You may later rearrange the paragraph for logic or style, but the credit will be in its proper place. After you have written the paper, do one last check, comparing notes and source materials to make sure that you haven't inadvertently slipped in a phrase or fact that you haven't given credit for. A good question to ask yourself is "Would the members of my class know this?" If the answer is "No," then the sentence needs a citation.

An Example of Plagiarism

To help you understand how to use research honestly, imagine that you are writing a paper about the uses of Greek mythology in the poetry of Percy Bysshe Shelley and one of your sources is the opening paragraph from Thomas Bulfinch's *The Age of Fable or Beauties of Mythology*:

> The religions of ancient Greece and Rome are extinct. The so-called divinities of Olympus have not a single worshipper among living men. They belong now not to the department of theology, but to those of literature and taste. There they still hold their place, and will continue to hold it, for they are too closely connected with the finest productions of poetry and art, both ancient and modern, to pass into oblivion.

> Bulfinch, Thomas. The Age of Fable or Beauties of Mythology. William H. Klapp, ed. New York: Tudor, 1935.

Here is an example of *deliberate plagiarism*:

> Although there is not a single living worshipper of the Greek or Roman gods, they will never pass into oblivion because they are too closely connected with the finest productions of poetry and art.

This sample should be totally revised—either to quote Bulfinch accurately or to paraphrase him. Either revision would still need to give credit to Bulfinch.

Here is an example of *careless plagiarism*:

> The Greek and Roman gods' close connection to the finest productions of poetry and art assure their continued place in civilization.

This sentence contains Bulfinch's idea and a rearrangement and minor modification of his phrases. It needs to be rephrased in the student's own words or put back in Bulfinch's exact phrases and then surrounded by quotation marks. Either variation will still need to be credited to Bulfinch.

Here is an example of *unconscious plagiarism*; the judgment—although not the phrasing—is from Bulfinch.

Even though no one believes in them today, I think that the Greek and Roman gods will always be important because they have inspired so much great art and literature.

In the example above, the student is paraphrasing Bulfinch's idea and must give credit for it. Here is the way the paraphrase should be credited:

Even though no one believes in them today, Bulfinch says that the Greek and Roman gods will always be important because they have inspired so much great art and literature (1).

Here is the way Bulfinch's exact words could be presented:

The Greek and Roman gods, according to Bulfinch, "are too closely connected with the finest productions of poetry and art, both ancient and modern, to pass into oblivion" (1).

The most important point to notice is that whether you quote or paraphrase, you always need to document your sources. Not to do so is *plagiarism—* whether *deliberate, careless,* or *unconscious.*

Chapter
14

Documentation: The MLA System for Parenthetical Citation

Imagine a friend reading the last version of your paper and asking a recurring question: "Where did you get this idea?" or "How do you know that this statistic is true?" Your answer, of course, is that for the most part you discovered the idea or statistic during your research. If you had to, you could find it on a particular page in an actual person's writing. In fact, providing this information is exactly what you're required to do in research papers. *Documentation* is the method that gives the sources of your information. All undocumented material in a research paper is presumed to be your own thoughts or experience.

You document the results of your research in two ways:

Citations
Works Cited

Citations are covered in this chapter and **Works Cited** are covered in the next chapter. As you are reporting material that you have discovered, you give citations in the paper to let the reader know the source—both to give authority to your paper and to avoid plagiarism. As you present material from your research, you should be explaining or reacting to it so that you won't have huge blocks of quotations or an uninterrupted series of citations. Document as gracefully as possible, by weaving in references to the authors smoothly, using running commentaries or transition words so that it is clear what is your idea or experience and what is your sources' (and from which source). Make sure that you have reviewed carefully the methods explained in chapter 11, "Varying the Way You Use Your Sources."

Material that Must Be Documented

In general, you will give credit for everything you learned during your research.

- facts
- statistics
- other people's words, ideas, or opinions

You do so whether you are quoting or using your own words. You do not give a source—even if you learned it during your research—for material that is general knowledge or is an obvious conclusion from the information. For example, you may not have known about the Chicago fire in 1871; you would need to give the source for any details you reported about it, but you wouldn't have to give credit for the fact that Chicago is in Illinois (which all readers should know) or for the judgment that the fire was devastating (which all readers would share), once you learned what had happened.

For English Classes, the MLA Style

The MLA (Modern Language Association) Style is the format most often used for documentation in scholarly publications and courses in English and foreign languages. Other disciplines use different formats, but unless you are given a specific style to follow for papers in an English or literature course, use the MLA Style.

This style places a brief reference or citation (the last name of the author and the page number) in parentheses immediately after you present any research information. At the end of the paper, a complete list of sources (*Works Cited*) provides the titles, dates, and other details about the particular books, articles, and other documents you used. This system has the advantage of acknowledging your sources as you present the information. Its disadvantage is that you have to learn how to punctuate around those parentheses.

Parenthetical Citation

Before we go into the details, let's look at a typical paragraph using parenthetical citations:*

Boys are taught assertiveness (even aggression) at a very young age to prove

their masculinity (Keen 38). Girls, however, are brought up to control their ag-

gressive feelings, and to prove their femininity by caring about others. Besides

being governed by different codes of behavior, according to Deborah Tannen,

the sexes "grow up in different worlds of words" (You Just Don't 43). The way

our society treats girls and boys while they are growing up explains the

problems that women and men have in communication (Tannen, That's Not).

These labels of what is "masculine" or what is "feminine" deny the fact that all

human beings have a range of feelings—sometimes needing to connect with

others and at other times needing to be independent or dominant. As Gloria

Steinem observes:

The little boy who is ridiculed for crying "like a girl" doesn't stop feeling sad,

he just buries that emotion; and the little girl who is punished for willfulness

as a "tomboy" just takes that spirit underground. (257)

*Bibliographical information for the sources mentioned in examples in this chapter can be found in the chart beginning on p. 132.

Notice how these citations have been used; they represent the most common forms:

- The first citation is after a paraphrase; it includes the last name of the author and the page number on which the original information appeared.

- The second citation is after a direct quotation of a phrase. Since the author was mentioned in the sentence, her last name is not given. However, a brief form of the title of her book (underlined or italicized) is given because, as the next citation makes clear, there are two books by this same author.

- The third citation requires the author's name because it has not been given in the sentence. However, the title of the book is also given to distinguish this citation from the one before. When no page is given, you know that the citation is for the whole work—in this case, Tannen's book.

- The last citation is after a direct quotation. The author's name introduced the quotation, so only the page number is needed. This quotation is set off ten spaces because it is longer than three lines.

You will notice that not only direct quotations require documentation. Summaries and paraphrases also require documentation.

After you have drafted your paper without looking at your notes (see pp. 79–80), go back, and with your notes beside you, add in the examples, facts, and other evidence that support your ideas. As you do so, insert in parentheses the last name of the person and the page number on which the quotation, opinion, or fact appeared.

MLA Format for Parenthetical Citations

- Place the last name of the author plus the page number inside parentheses.

- Do not use "p" or "pg" for "page"; just give the number.

- For a short quotation or paraphrase incorporated into a line of your paragraph, do not punctuate before the opening parenthesis. Place a period outside the second parenthesis, unless you are continuing your sentence.

Both boys and girls have masculine and feminine sides (Steinem 257).

- For a long quotation (more than three lines) that is set off, end the quotation with a period and then place the citation in parentheses without a period.

The little boy who is ridiculed for crying "like a girl" doesn't stop feeling sad, he just buries that emotion; and the little girl who is punished for willfulness as a "tomboy" just takes that spirit underground. (Steinem 257)

If you have already introduced the author's name, just give the page number in parentheses.

Wendell Berry defends his resistance to the technology of word processing (67).

If you are citing a work that has two or three authors, give all last names, joined by "and."

"A B-type star is an object exhibiting neutral helium lines in its spectrum, but no ionized helium lines" (Jaschek and Jaschek 136).

Synthesized marijuana is used to treat asthma and to control nausea during chemotherapy (Jaffe, Petersen, and Hodgson 78).

If you are citing a work that has four or more authors, give the last name of the first one only, plus *et al.* ["and others"]:

Advocates need to learn how to "address the child's fears without making them worse" (Duquette et al., 79).

If you are citing a work that has no author listed, give the first important word of the title. Note that it cannot be a word (such as the name of your topic) common to other titles on your *Works Cited* page: the reader has to be able to recognize your reference.

Time reports that the majority of colleges and universities now have banned smoking from large areas—even entire buildings ("Kicking Butts" 71).

If you are using two or more works by the same author in your paper, give the author's name, a brief version of the title, and the page number. Underline, italicize, or quote the title as appropriate. (See p. 101.)

Men and women have different purposes while engaging in conversation (Tannen, You Just Don't 77).

Lewis Thomas hopes that we could then "regain the kind of spontaneity and zest for ideas" lost when we try to understand every thought, memory, or dream ("The Attic of the Brain" 40).

If you are using a quotation that your source has quoted, identify in your sentence who actually said it or wrote it. Then in your citation use the phrase "qtd. in" [for *quoted in*].

Scott Eckert has recorded the deep dives of the leatherback turtle, and gives it "a tentative 400-foot lead" over the diving record of the sperm whale (qtd. in "Up Front" 14).

Deconstructionism, according to Helen Gardner, is an approach "partly justified by being linked with a universal skepticism about the possibility of any real knowledge of the universe we live in . . ." (qtd. in Thomas, Late Night Thoughts 68–69).

If you are referring to an interview or lecture, do not use a parenthetical citation. Instead, mention the name of the interviewee or speaker and his or her job title and how you heard the information.

In an interview, Max Sherman, the Dean of the Lyndon B. Johnson School for Public Affairs at the University of Texas, said that the proposal is worthy of consideration.

If you are using an unusual source that doesn't fit any of the patterns given above, give enough information in your sentence so the reader will recognize the source in the *Works Cited* page.

The 1939 version of the film presents the moors of <u>Wuthering Heights</u> as a private playground for Catherine and Heathcliff.

After you have finished writing your paper and have incorporated the citations of your sources, you are ready to prepare the last page of your paper, the *Works Cited* page. In the next chapter, we will explain how to compose your *Works Cited* page. For a student paper using parenthetical citations and a *Works Cited* page according to the MLA Style, see the appendix.

Chapter 15

Documentation: The MLA System for *Works Cited*

While you were taking notes, you should have kept a separate list of the names, titles, and dates of your sources in a safe place—your "working bibliography." Many items on that list will make up your *Works Cited* page. If you also typed your list into a word processor in the correct format, you have already saved yourself a great deal of work. If you have your working bibliography on cards, your next step is to alphabetize and type from those cards. Whatever method you used, you now need to prepare a list for your *Works Cited* page.

Go through the entire paper and note the names or titles of the sources you mentioned when you were reporting the results of your research. Most of those sources will have a parenthetical citation, but be sure to include references for sources that do not get parenthetical citations—persons you interviewed and institutions you visited.

At the end of your paper, you must list your actual references for the information given within the paper—all the sources you cited.

Remember to avoid these pitfalls:

- You cannot include a source in the list of *Works Cited* if you didn't refer to it in your paper. Delete from your working bibliography any source that you didn't actually use.

- If you have a source that you know you took information from but you have no citation for it, backtrack through your notes from that source till you find what you used, and then find the corresponding information in your paper. Add the appropriate parenthetical citation in the paper, and add that source to your list of *Works Cited*.

- You list a source whether you used it extensively or just once—and whether you used quotations from it, or paraphrased it, or summarized it.

Content of the *Works Cited* Page

For each source in your *Works Cited* page, make sure that you have:

- The complete name of the author(s)
- The complete title, including the subtitle
- The date of publication or release
- The title of the article and the pages covered if you are using only part of the publication

In addition, for *books, pamphlets,* or *brochures:*

- The publisher and city of publication
- The name of the editor if any
- The number of the edition if not the first

In addition, for *newspaper articles:*

- The section letter or number if any

In addition, for articles in a *scholarly journal:*

- The volume number

In addition, full details for *unusual sources:*

- The location of a lecture or interview
- The running time of a film

General Format of the *Works Cited* Page

Format details—*arrangement, punctuation,* and *spacing*—are an important part of the formal presentation of academic research. Many teachers look first at the format of your documentation, so paying attention to these guidelines will assure a favorable first impression—and may affect the grade of your paper.

- Do not separate items by type (for example, books and articles), unless asked to do so.
- Do not number the items. Instead, list each item on a new line, beginning at the left margin. Continue the first line all the way to the right margin, and then indent the other lines five spaces each from the left margin.

- Alphabetize the entire list by the last name of author, editor, artist, or speaker. If no author is given, alphabetize using the first major word of the title. If the author is an organization, alphabetize by the first main word of the organization.

A sample *Works Cited* page appears on page 194.

Format for Authors' Names

- One author
  List the last name, followed by a comma, and then list the first name.

  Tsai, Henry. The Chinese Experience. Bloomington: Indiana UP, 1986.

- Two or three authors
  Reverse the name of only the first author if there are more than one.

  Burka, Jane B., and Lenora M. Yuen. Procrastination: Why You Do It,

     What to Do About It. Toronto: Addison, 1983.

  Fagen, Richard, Richard Brody, and Thomas O'Leary. Cubans in Exile.

     Stanford, CA: Stanford UP, 1968.

- Four or more authors
  If there are four or more authors, list only the first one as given on the title page, followed by the abbreviation **et al.** [meaning "and others"].

  Bentson, George J., et al. Perspectives on Safe and Sound Banking.

     Cambridge, MA: MIT, 1986.

- Same author for two or more works
  If you have used two or more works from the same author, alphabetize by the first main word of each title and list the author's name for only the first work. *Use three hyphens and a period* in place of the author's name for the second work. Give all other bibliographical information for each work—even if some of the information is the same.

  Tannen, Deborah. That's Not What I Meant! New York: Ballantine,

     1986.

  ---. You Just Don't Understand: Women and Men in Conversation.

     New York: Ballantine, 1990.

- No author
  If the author is not named, alphabetize by the first main word of the title of the article or booklet.

  "Smoking Laws: After the Air War." Governing Aug. 1991: 23–24.

Format for Titles

- Capitalize the first letter of the first word and of all the main words of the title—even if they were not capitalized in the original source. Do not use all capitals, even if they were used in the source.

- Leave one space after every comma, two spaces after every period and colon.

- Italicize or underline with an unbroken line the titles of any work published by itself—books; magazines; newspapers; brochures or pamphlets; films; recordings; and computer, television, or radio programs.

  Jaschek, Carlos, and Mercedes Jaschek. The Classification of the Stars.

  New York: Cambridge UP, 1987.

  Shot in Hollywood. Videocassette. Carousel, 1986. 16 min.

- Surround with double quotation marks the titles of short works that are published inside larger works—articles, chapters, stories, essays, poems, songs, and cartoons.

  "Curiosity Killed the Bat." Natural History Nov. 1989: 62.

  Dorman, Michael. "Who Killed Medgar Evers?" New York Times 17

  May 1992, sec. 6: 52+.

- Use a colon after the main title to introduce a subtitle.

  Keen, Sam. Fire in the Belly: On Being a Man. New York: Bantam,

  1991.

- Put a period after the title. If the title ends with a question mark or exclamation point, you don't need a period.

  Tannen, Deborah. That's Not What I Meant! New York: Ballantine,

  1986.

Format for Publishers' Information

- Do not give publishers' information for newspapers, magazines, encyclopedias, or dictionaries.

- For books, give the city of publication. If several cities are listed on the title page, list the first one. Give the postal service two-letter abbreviation for the state unless the city is generally known.

    Benardete, Doris, ed. <u>Mark Twain: Wit and Wisecracks</u>. Mount Ver-

    non, NY: Peter Pauper, 1961.

- Follow the city by a colon, then two spaces, then the brief name of the publisher, without labels such as "Inc.," and "Co.," or "Publishers." Abbreviate "University Press" as UP without periods.

    Fagen, Richard, Richard Brody, and Thomas O'Leary. <u>Cubans in Exile</u>.

    Stanford, CA: Stanford UP, 1968.

    Flagg, Fannie. <u>Fried Green Tomatoes at the Whistle Stop Cafe</u>. New

    York: McGraw, 1988.

    Zipes, Jack. <u>Breaking the Magic Spell: Radical Theories of Folk and</u>

    <u>Fairy Tales</u>. Austin: U of Texas P, 1979.

- Follow the name of the publisher with a comma and then the most recent date of revision or copyright as listed on the back of the title page. If the book has been re-published, put the original date of publication after the title and the date of the edition you used at the end.

    Chopin, Kate. <u>The Awakening</u>. 1899. New York: Avon, 1972.

- End each bibliographic item with a period.

Specific Applications

Books (except dictionaries or encyclopedias)

Grossvogel, David I. <u>Mystery and Its Fictions</u>. Baltimore: Johns

Hopkins UP, 1979.

- List the author, last name first, followed by a comma, then the first name followed by the middle name or initial if any, followed by a period.

- Then list the title, underlined; if there is a subtitle, it is listed after the title with a colon. Follow the title with a period.

- Next give the city of publication followed by a colon, two spaces, and then the short name of the publisher, without "Company," or "Inc.," or "Publishers."

- Follow the publisher's name with a comma, a space, and the most recent date of copyright (given on the back of the title page).

- End the entry with a period.

Essay or Chapter in an Edited Book

Atwood, Margaret. "Homelanding." A Writer's Reader. Ed. Donald

Hall and D. L. Emblem. 6th ed. New York: HarperCollins, 1991,

32–34.

- Give the author of the piece you used (last name first), followed by a period.

- Then list the title of the essay or chapter in quotation marks, with a period before the closing quotation mark.

- Then give the title of the book, underlined and followed by a period.

- Next write **Ed.** [for editor or editors] and the name of the editor(s) of the book, first name first, followed by a period.

- Give all the remaining publication information, in the same format as for other books, but place a comma after the date.

- Add the pages covered by the article (just the numbers, with no "p." or "pg.") and end with a period.

Article in a Scholarly Journal, Popular Magazine, or Newspaper

- Author's name: First list the author's name, last name first, followed by a period and two spaces.

Lew, Julie. "Invisibility Is More than Meets the Eye." New York Times

23 Feb. 1992, sec. 2: 26.

- No author: If there is no author listed, begin with the title of the article.

  "The Effect of Cigarette Smoking on Hemoglobin Levels and Anemia

    Screening." Journal of the American Medical Association 264

    (26 Sept. 1990): 1556-64.

- Title of article: Give the title of the article in quotation marks, with a period before the closing quotation mark. Follow with two spaces.

  Straits, Bruce C. "The Social Context of Voter Turnout." Public Opinion

    Quarterly 30 (Spring 1990): 64-73.

- Title of periodical: Give the title of the magazine or newspaper, underlined, followed by a space and no punctuation.

  Ferris, Timothy. "The Year The Warning Lights Flashed On: Disasters

    of High Technology from the Past, Present and Maybe the

    Future." Life Jan. 1987: 67-71.

- Volume number: Do *not* give the volume or issue number for newspapers or popular magazines. *Do* give the volume number for scholarly journals.

  Crouse, James, and Dale Trusheim. "How Colleges Can Correctly

    Determine Selection Benefits from the SAT." Harvard Education

    Review 61 (May 1991): 125-47.

  Smith, Marguerite T. "Slashing the Taxes on Your Home." Money

    Jan. 1993: 96-100.

- Date of publication: Give the date of the publication in the following order: day, month (abbreviated), and year—with no commas between them, but with a colon and two spaces after the year.

  Biedny, David. "Aldus Gallery Effects." MacUser Apr. 1992: 58-70.

  Seligman, Daniel. "Liberal Poker." Fortune 6 May 1991: 115.

- For a scholarly journal, put the date in parentheses after the volume number.

  Berry, Wendell. "The Body and the Machine." <u>Parabola</u> 15 (Fall 1990):

  66–74.

- Section of newspaper: After the date of a newspaper, insert a comma and give the edition or section number if any, abbreviating as *ed.* or *sec.*, with the number (in arabic numerals) or capitalized letter, followed by a colon, plus two spaces.
  If the section is identified by a letter, do not use *sec;* simply put the letter before the page number.

  Brody, Jane E. "Encouraging Statistics on Breast Cancer." <u>New York</u>

  <u>Times</u> 14 Oct 1992: C14.

  Finn, Robin. "Russian Qualifies as a Wimbledon Giant-Killer." <u>New</u>

  <u>York Times</u> 28 June 1992, sec. 8: 1–2.

- <u>Pages:</u> Give the pages covered by the article.
  —Use a hyphen to indicate consecutive pages.
  —List no more than the last two digits of the second number if the number will be clear:
    23–29
    114–18
    179–202
    1556–64
  —Use a comma for two separate pages (23, 29).
  —For over two non-continuous pages, use a plus sign (23+).

  Dorman, Michael. "Who Killed Medgar Evers?" <u>New York Times</u> 17

  May 1992, sec. 6: 52+.

Nonprint Sources

When you cite nonprint sources, follow the guidelines for the format of books. Give enough information that the reader of your paper could find the source.

- For an audiocassette, compact disc, or record, give the artist, title (underlined), format and producer of that particular format, plus the date of production.

  R.E.M. <u>Automatic for the People</u>. Compact disc. Warner, 1992.

- For a computer program, give the name of the writer if known, the title of the program (underlined), the version (preceded by the abbreviation *Vers.*), the producer, date, and computer specifications.

LabanWriter. Vers. 3.0. Computer software. Ohio State University,

  1990–92. Macintosh, disk.

- For a film, give the director, the title (underlined), format and producer of that particular format, plus the date of original production and the running time.

Kurosawa, Akira. Ran. Videocassette. CBS/Fox, 1985. 160 min.

- For a radio or television program, give the name of the person you quoted or paraphrased, the title of the program (underlined), the station or network, and the date of original broadcast.

Angle, Jim. Marketplace. NPR [National Public Radio]. 12 Jan. 1993.

- For a work of art, give the artist, the title of the work (underlined), and information on where you saw it.

McKim, Mead and White. Pennsylvania Station. Photograph in Na-

  than Silver. Lost New York. New York: Schocken, 1971, 33–38.

O'Keeffe, Georgia. Black Iris 1926. Metropolitan Museum, Alfred

  Stieglitz Collection, New York.

Unusual Sources or Missing Information

In general, it is better to give too much information about an unusual source (one not found readily in libraries) than to be cautious about format. When a source does not fit into any of the guidelines presented here, follow the format for a book. Give enough data about the publisher (if known) that the reader of your paper could actually find that source.

Berger, Bruce. "Dancing with Time." American Way [American

  Airlines] 15 Feb. 1992, 40+.

Jengo, Jay. "25 Years of Star Trek." The Inside Collector [Northport,

  NY] May 1992: 57–62.

- Missing information: Use the following abbreviations to denote missing information:

  n.d.   for *no date of publication given.*

  n.p.   for either *no place of publication* or *no publisher* listed

  n.pag.   for *no page numbers given.*

Federal Trade Commission. <u>Building a Better Credit Record</u>. Washing-

   ton: GPO, n.d.

John, Nicholas. "Fatal Attractions: Carmen and Her Admirers." <u>Car-</u>

   <u>men Jones</u>. [Playbill at the Old Vic Theatre]. London: 1991.

   n.pag.

- When very little information is available about the document, indicate in brackets whatever details you can deduce, adding a question mark if this is an educated guess on your part. If they are numbered, give the number of pages to indicate the length of the source.

Cultural Assistance Center [for the Commission for Cultural Affairs of

   the City of New York]. <u>A Guide to New York City Museums</u>.

   1977. n.pag.

<u>Little Italy: Souvenir Book</u>. [New York]: n.p. [1983?]. 32 pp.

The following page is an example of a *Works Cited* page taken from a study of whales by a student, Thomas Sperandeo. For a complete documented paper using the MLA Style, see the appendix, p. 189.

A Sample of a *Works Cited* Page

Works Cited

"Ban on Whaling Saved." Greenpeace Sept./Oct. 1990: 22.

"Buying Sanctuary: A Permanent Way to Save the Whale." The
Economist 22 June 1991: 43–46.

Corrigan, Patricia. Where the Whales Are: Your Guide to Whale-
Watching Trips in North America. Pequot, CT: Globe, 1991.

Durrell, Lee. State of the Ark: An Atlas of Conservation in Action.
Garden City: Doubleday, 1986.

Ellis, Richard. Men and Whales. New York: Knopf, 1991.

Gardner, Robert. The Whale Watcher's Guide. New York: Penguin,
1984.

Martin, Richard Mark. Mammals of the Ocean. New York: Putnam,
1977.

"Oppose Commercial Whaling." Greenpeace June 1991: 24.

"Race for the Whales." Greenpeace Mar. 1991: 26+.

Stonehouse, Bernard. Saving the Animals: The World Wildlife Fund
Book of Conservation. New York: Macmillan, 1981.

"Whale Populations Take a Dive." Environment Aug. 1989: 37+.

"Whales." Encyclopedia Britannica. 17th ed.

"Whaling." Collier's Encyclopedia. 20th ed.

Note: Your Works Cited *will not follow the order of this chart. See the sample on p. 131.*

Annotated Chart of Sample

Source	Information Needed
Article in a magazine	Author. "Title of Article." Title of Journal or Magazine Date: pages covered.
Article in a newspaper	Author. "Title of Article." Title of Newspaper Date, sec. [for section, if any]: pages covered.
Article in a scholarly journal	Author. "Title of Article." Title of Journal Volume number (Date): pages covered.
Article with no author listed	"Title of Article." Title of Newspaper or Magazine Date, sec. [for section, if any]: pages covered.
Book—one author	Author [last name, first name]. Title of Book. City of Publication: Publisher, latest date of copyright.
Book or article, same author as for entry above	---. [three hyphens and a period, no spaces in between] Alphabetize by title. [Give all information as for any other work, even if there is repetition.]
Book—two authors	First Author [last name, first name], Second Author [first name last name]. Title of Book. City of Publication: Publisher, latest date of copyright.
Book—three authors	First Author [last name, first name], Second Author [first name last name], Third Author [first name last name]. Title of Book. City of Publication: Publisher, latest date of copyright.
Book—more than three authors or editors	First Author or Editor listed on title page [last name, first name], et al. [for "and others"]. Title of Book. City of Publication: Publisher, latest date of copyright.

Entries for a *Works Cited* Page

Sample Entries

Lorenzini, Beth. "University of Michigan Seeks Grant to Step Up Recycling Efforts." <u>Restaurants and Institutions</u> 1 May 1991: 13.

Dorman, Michael. "Who Killed Medgar Evers?" <u>New York Times</u> 17 May 1992, sec. 6: 52+.

Margolis, Stephen E. "Monopolistic Competition and Multiproduct Brand Names." <u>Journal of Business</u> 62 (April 1989): 199–209.

"Up Front: Yertle: 1 Orca: 0." <u>Discover</u> Sept. 1987: 14.

Tannen, Deborah. <u>That's Not What I Meant!</u> New York: Ballantine, 1986.

---. <u>You Just Don't Understand: Women and Men in Conversation</u>. New York: Ballantine, 1990.

Jaschek, Carlos, and Mercedes Jaschek. <u>The Classification of the Stars</u>. New York: Cambridge UP, 1987.

Jaffe, Jerome, Robert Petersen, and Ray Hodgson. <u>Addictions: Issues and Answers</u>. New York: Harper, 1980.

Duquette, Donald N., et al. <u>Advocating for the Child in Protection Proceedings: A Handbook for Lawyers and Court-Appointed Special Advocates</u>. Lexington, MA: Lexington, 1990.

Annotated Chart of Sample

Source	Information Needed
Book with editor (no author listed)	Editor [last name, first name], ed. [for editor]. Title of Book. City of Publication: Publisher, latest date of copyright.
Book, not first edition	Author or Editor, ed. [for editor if necessary]. Title of Book. Number of edition [written in digit plus suffix]. City of Publication: Publisher, latest date of copyright.
Book with both editor and author	Author [last name, first name]. Title of Book. Ed. [for editor] Editor's name [first name first]. City of Publication: Publisher, latest date of copyright.
Book with organization as author	Name of Organization in normal order. Title of Book. City of Publication: Publisher [even if it is the same as the organization], latest date of copyright.
Book review or other work	Reviewer's name [last name, first name]. "Title of the Review." Rev. [for "review"] of Title of Work Reviewed, by name of author or artist [first name first]. Title of Magazine or Newspaper Date: pages covered.
Chapter or essay in edited book	Author of Chapter or Essay [last name, first name]. "Title of Chapter." Title of Book. Ed. [for editor] Name of Editor [first name first]. City of Publication: Publisher, latest copyright date, numbers of the pages covered.
Editorial or cartoon	Author if given. "Title" if given. Editorial [or Cartoon]. Title of periodical. Date: page.
Encyclopedia article	"Title of Article." Title of Encyclopedia. Number of edition [digit plus suffix].

Entries for a *Works Cited* Page

Rushing, Brian C., ed. 1990 Internships: 38,000 On-the-Job Training
    Opportunities for College Students and Adults. Cincinnati:
    Writer's Digest, 1989.

Perrine, Laurence. Sound and Sense: An Introduction to Poetry. 7th ed.
    San Diego: Harcourt, 1987.

Bulfinch, Thomas. The Art of Fable, or Beauties of Mythology. Ed.
    William H. Klapp. New York: Tudor, 1935.

Federal Trade Commission. Building a Better Credit Record.
    Washington: GPO, n.d.

Rubin, Hanna. "The City's Front Yard." Rev. of A Year in Central Park,
    by Laurie A. Walters. New York Times 25 Oct. 1992, sec. 6: 20.

Atwood, Margaret. "Homelanding." A Writer's Reader. Ed. Donald
    Hall and D. L. Emblem. 6th ed. New York: HarperCollins, 1991,
    32–34.

Richter, Mischa. Cartoon. New Yorker 23 Mar. 1992: 37.

"Biblical Literature and Its Critical Interpretation." Encyclopaedia
    Britannica: Macropaedia. 15th ed.

Source	Information Needed
Government publication	Author or Agency. <u>Title of Publication</u>. Washington: GPO [for Government Printing Office], date.
Interview	Name of Interviewee. Interviewee's Job Title. Personal [or telephone] interview. City. Date.
Radio or television program	Presenter(s) of the Information. <u>Title of Program</u>. Network [if any]. Call Letters of Broadcasting Station. Date of Broadcast.
Videocassette, audiotape, compact disc, or computer program	Artist or Author. <u>Title</u>. Videocassette [or other format]. Production Company, date. Running time or engineering specifics.

Entries for a *Works Cited* Page

Sample Entries

National Governors' Association. <u>Results in Education: State-Level
  College Assessment Initiatives—1987–88: Results of a Fifty-State
  Survey</u>. Washington: GPO, 1985.

Sherman, Max. Dean, Lyndon Baines Johnson School of Public Affairs.
  Personal Interview. Austin, TX. 21 Oct. 1992.

Moyers, Bill, and Robert Bly. <u>A Gathering of Men</u>. Public
  Broadcasting System. WNET TV. 8 Jan. 1990.

Wyler, William. <u>Wuthering Heights</u>. Videocassette. CBS Fox, 1939.
  118 min.

Chapter 16

Documentation: Four Other Systems You Might Need

In chapters 14 and 15, we have given the currently favored format for documentation, the MLA (Modern Language Association) Style, used in English classes and for scholarly publications for English and foreign languages. However, there are other choices, depending on your audience and discipline. This chapter explains how to document your research using four other systems:

- The Classic Style: Footnotes and Bibliography

- A Variation: Endnotes

- For Social Sciences and Natural Sciences: The APA Style

- For Physical Sciences: The ACS System

All four systems give the same basic information to identify the source, but the punctuation and arrangement of the information are different.

You will find that particular academic disciplines use variations of these formats. Ask your instructor which style to use.

The Classic Style: Footnotes and Bibliography

This traditional system is the best choice for a report for a general audience or for courses in art, communications, dance, journalism, music, theater, history, or political science.

With footnotes, you place a raised numeral in your paper every time you present information from your research—either at the end of the summary, paraphrase, or quotation (after the quotation marks), or within the sentence, right after the fact or statistic. The raised numeral is then repeated at the bottom of that page (see the example below), with the specific source of the information. MLA formerly used this system, and they still explain how to do it.[1]

The numbers for this footnoting system are continuous; that is, you begin with the number one and progress, using the next number each time you document a fact or quotation from your research. Thus, one source may be referred to several times, but each new use of material from that source will have a new number. After the first complete footnote, subsequent footnotes for that source give only the last name of the author and the appropriate page number.[2]

The advantages of this system are that

- If readers are curious about the source, they can easily glance down to the bottom of the page.

- The writer of the paper can make interpretive or explanatory comments.[3]

The disadvantage is that you have to plan carefully so that the number in the text and the correspondingly numbered footnote are on the same page. Computers, however, simplify this task. In fact, once you learn how easy this system for documentation is with a computer, you may prefer to use it for certain projects. Check with your teacher to make sure that this is an acceptable format.

Format for Footnotes

- Footnotes begin at the bottom of the page—four lines below the last line of text—and correspond to the numbers given in the text on that page.

- First draw a two-inch line (twelve strokes of the underline key) and skip a line.

- Indent five spaces and give the appropriate raised numeral.

- Give the name of the author first name first.

- Follow the author's name with a comma and a space.

---

[1] Joseph Gibaldi and Walter S. Achtert, <u>MLA Handbook for Writers of Research Papers</u> 3rd ed. (New York: MLA, 1988), 183–200.

[2] Gibaldi and Achtert, 200.

[3] The footnote can add a comment that would otherwise clutter up your paper.

ADBF CP - APA
(ABC, PD)

- *For books:*
  - Give the title, underlined, followed by a space but no punctuation.
  - After an opening parenthesis, give first the city of publication, followed by a colon and two spaces.
  - Then give the name of the publisher, followed by a comma and one space.
  - Give the date of copyright, then a closing parenthesis, followed by a comma, then a space.
  - Give the page number(s), without *p.* or *pp.*
  - End the entry with a period.

[4]Joseph Gibaldi and Walter S. Achtert, MLA Handbook for Writers of Research Papers 3rd ed. (New York: MLA, 1988), 183–200.

- *For articles:* (AAM, VIP)
  - Give the title of the article in quotation marks, with a comma inside the closing quotation marks.
  - After one space, give the title of the periodical, underlined and followed by no punctuation.
  - Give the volume number for scholarly journals and enclose the date in parentheses, followed by a comma.
  - Give the date of the periodical—day, month, and year with no punctuation and one space between—followed by a colon and two spaces.
  - Give the page number(s) followed by a period.

[5]Lynn Veach Sadler, "Spinsters, Non-Spinsters, and Men in the World of Barbara Pym," Critique 30 (Spring 1985), 141–154.

Formerly, the footnote method relied on Latin abbreviations, but only one is used regularly today: You may use <u>ibid</u>. [meaning "the same"] plus the page number in a footnote for the same reference as the one preceding it. However, it is also correct—and easier—to give only the author's last name and the specific page number once you have cited a source completely.

Here is an example of a paragraph using footnotes. Check the numerals and the matching footnotes at the bottom of the page:

Frank Campion analyzes how health insurance changed the way Americans pay doctors and hospitals. After the institution of Medicaid and Medicare, medical costs "rose rapidly."[6] At the same time, insurance "substantially reduced and in some cases eliminated out of pocket cost for all but 10–15 percent of the population."[7]

---

[6]Frank Campion, The AMA and U.S. Health Policy since 1940 (Chicago: Chicago Review P, 1984), 507.

[7]ibid., 506.

Bibliography

The *Bibliography*, at the end of the paper, is a list of all the sources referred to in the footnotes. Each source is listed only once—in alphabetical order by the authors' last names (not in the order you used them), and in the same format as for the *Works Cited* page, already given in the previous chapter.

Because the information is the same for both footnotes and bibliography (only in a slightly different format), some teachers will allow you to skip the bibliography for a short paper using footnotes. Check with your instructor.

In addition, this system allows you to list a *Supplementary Bibliography*—a list of sources that you read for background or tangential information, but did not actually use to write the report.

A student paper using the classic footnote and bibliography style, "A Parent's Reading of 'Hansel and Gretel,'" by Donna Pesiri, appears on pp. 194+ in the appendix. You may want to compare it to the same paper using the MLA Style.

A Variation: Endnotes

This system is the same as the footnote system, except the footnotes are moved from the foot of each page and are instead accumulated in numerical order at the end of the paper on a separate page, called *Notes*. This method simplifies the typing, but it has a disadvantage for the reader who must leaf back and forth to check the sources.

Format for Endnotes

- After the title, *Notes* (centered), skip two lines and indent the first line five spaces.
- Give the raised numeral.
- Skip a space and then begin the note.
- Use the same format as for footnotes (see p. 139).
- Double-space the entire page.

For an example of a paper using endnotes and a bibliography, see pages 201–206 in the appendix.

For Social Sciences and Natural Sciences: The APA Style

The APA (American Psychological Association) Style for reporting research is quite similar to the MLA Style, except it emphasizes the date of publication—both in the parenthetical citations and in the list of references at the end. Use this system for papers in the social sciences or the natural sciences.

Citations

With this method, both the name of the author and the date are given in the paper whenever information is presented. Here are the most common forms:

> Keen (1991) described how masculinity and aggression are intertwined in American social values.

> The way our society treats girls and boys while they are growing up explains the problems that women and men have in communication (Tannen 1986).

The preferred way is to use the author's last name in your sentence:

> Tannen (1990) contrasted the American cultural rearing of girls and boys.

Note that in APA Style, the author's work is described in the past tense ("contrasted").

For a direct quotation—but not for a paraphrase—the page number is also given, with the abbreviation "p." or "pp." Here is a paragraph using the APA Style:

> Keen (1991) described how boys are taught assertiveness (even aggression) at a very young age to prove their masculinity. Girls, however, are brought up to control their aggressive feelings, and to prove their femininity by caring about others. Besides being governed by different codes of behavior, according to Tannen (1990), the sexes "grow up in different worlds of words" (p. 43). The way our society treats girls and boys while they are growing up explains the problems that women and men have in communication (Tannen 1986). These labels of what is "masculine" or what is "feminine" deny the fact that all human beings have a range of feelings—sometimes needing to connect with others and at other times needing to be independent or dominant. As Steinem (1992) observed:
>> The little boy who is ridiculed for crying "like a girl" doesn't stop feeling sad, he just buries that emotion; and the little girl who is punished for willfulness as a "tomboy" just takes that spirit underground (p. 257).

Notice how these citations have been used; they represent the most common forms:

- The first citation includes only the date; the name of the author has already been given, and this is a paraphrase so you don't need a page number.

- The second citation gives the date after the author's name, indicating which work is cited.

- The third citation is after a direct quotation of a phrase. Since the author and date have already been given, only the page number is necessary.

- The fourth citation requires the author's name because it has not been given in the sentence. No page number is given, because this is not a direct quotation. The date, 1986, tells you that this is a different book by Tannen.

- The fifth citation gives the date of Steinem's book.

- The last citation is after a direct quotation. The author's name introduced the quotation, so only the page number is needed. This quotation is set off because it's longer than three lines.

References — *ADBE CP*

The APA Style follows all the rules that we have already given for the *Works Cited* page according to the MLA system (see chap. 15), with these exceptions:

- The list is called *References.*

- Give only the initials for the first and middle names of authors, and give all names in reverse order—even for multiple authors. List all authors up to six (and then use et al.).

Jaffe, J., Petersen, R., & Hodgson, R. (1980). <u>Addictions: Issues and</u>

<u>answers</u>. New York: Harper & Row.

Duquette, D. N., et al. (1990). <u>Advocating for the child in protection</u>

<u>proceedings: A handbook for lawyers and court-appointed special</u>

<u>advocates</u>. Lexington, MA: Lexington Books.

- The year for each entry is moved up and placed within parentheses—right after the author's name:

Steinem, G. (1992). <u>Revolution from within: A book of self esteem</u>.

    Boston: Little Brown.

- When listing an author with two or more books with the same date, distinguish among the works by adding a letter to the date—for example, 1990a, 1990b, 1990c.

Mindell, A. (1985a). <u>River's way</u>. London: Routledge & Kegan Paul.

Mindell, A. (1985b). <u>Working with the dreaming body</u>. London: Rout-

    ledge & Kegan Paul.

- For articles, the month and day are placed in parentheses following the year. Do not abbreviate the month.

Yang, J. E. (1987, June 15). Fraud is main cause of failure at S & Ls in

    California, congressional study says. <u>Wall Street Journal</u>, p. 6.

- Capitalize only the first word of titles and subtitles, and any proper names, for books, encyclopedias, and articles, but capitalize all main words of newspapers, magazines and scholarly journals.

Curiosity killed the bat. (1989, November). <u>Natural History</u>, p. 62.

- Do not use quotation marks around the titles of articles, essays, and chapters. (Do underline the titles of books, newspapers, and magazines.)

Dorman, M. Who killed Medgar Evers? <u>New York Times</u>, sec. 6,

    pp. 52+.

- Use *p.* or *pp.* to indicate the page number(s) for articles in magazines and newspapers, or for chapters in books.

Stevenson, J. (1992, September 21). Food for naught. <u>New Republic</u>,

    pp. 13–14, 16.

- For scholarly journals, give the volume number underlined, followed by a comma and then the page number(s) (no *p.* or *pp.*).

Margolis, S. E. (1989, April). Monopolistic competition and multiprod-

uct brand names. Journal of Business, 62, 199–209.

- Do not abbreviate publishers' names; do abbreviate *and* with &.

Burka, J. B., & Yuen, L. (1983). *Procrastination: Why you do it, what to*

do about it. Toronto: Addison Wesley.

For a complete paper using APA Style, see the appendix, pages 207–217.

For Physical Sciences: The ACS System

The American Chemical Society (ACS) system is used in mathematics, chemistry, and physics.

Citations

- Each source reference is given a number in the order of appearance in the paper.
- The number for the source is repeated in the text every time the source is credited for information.
- In the text, the numbers are raised, like footnote numbers.

A good presentation of how these principles operate in computer-assisted design is Leendert Ammeraal's description of "finite solid objects that are essentially bounded flat faces."[7]

- The numbers match up with the list of references at the end of the paper.
- Multiple numbers indicate that the respectively numbered sources agree or have data on that point. Use a comma (,) to mean "and" and use a hyphen (-) to mean "through."

There are also options that allow you to make an image look as if wind were blowing it away or as if it were made up of tiles.[2-5]

References

For every entry

- List sources (and number them only once) in the order in which they are referred to in the paper—rather than in alphabetical order as with other systems. Thus, number one is the source mentioned first in the paper, no matter how often it is again referred to; number four is the fourth new reference in the paper.

- Begin at the left margin with the number for each entry enclosed in parentheses, without a period.
- Indent five spaces for every line (block format).
- End each entry with a period.

(1)   Ferris, T. Life **1987** 10 (1), 67–7.

Authors

- Reverse all the authors' names and give only initials for first and middle names; use semicolons between the names. List all multiple authors.

(2)   Jaschek, C.; Jaschek, M. "The Classification of the Stars". Cambridge: New York, **1987**.

Books

- Put quotation marks around the titles of books, and place the period outside the quotation marks.
- Give the name of the publisher, followed by a colon and two spaces, then the city of publication followed by a comma and one space.
- Boldface the date or underline it with a wavy line.

(3)   Brossi, A., Ed. "Alkaloids: Chemistry and Pharmacology". Academic P: San Diego, **1990**.

Articles

- Do not give the title of the article for journal articles.
- Abbreviate and underline the title of the journal, followed by the year (boldfaced or underlined with a wavy line but without punctuation), followed by a space, and then the volume number, no space, the issue number in parentheses, a comma, no space, and then the page numbers.

(4)   Hsu, J. P.; Schattenberg, H. J., III; Garza, M. M. J. Assoc. of Anal. Chem. **1991** 74(5),886–892.

Here is a paragraph by Eric Jergenson, a student, using ACS citations, followed by his *References* page.

In 1837, Dr. C. G. Page of Salem, Massachusetts, was experimenting with a primitive battery, a coil, and some horseshoe magnets.[1] He knew that the wet-cell battery, invented by Volta in 1800,[2] stored an electrical charge and was capable of furnishing an electric current. Page also knew that electric currents flow due to voltage, which is an electrical pressure, through an electrical circuit.[2-3] What Page was not aware of was the properties of coils or the concept of induction, the process by which a body with electrical or magnetic properties creates similar properties in a neighboring body without direct contact.[2-3] When the coil was attached to the battery and one or both poles of the magnet were placed by the coil, a ringing sound was heard in the magnet when connections to the battery were either made or broken. Page believed that the sound was the reverberation of the snapping sound made when connections to the battery were made or broken.[1] Actually, the coil became magnetized by the flow of current from the battery and through electromagnetic induction, the magnets were caused to vibrate whenever the circuit was made or broken.[2-3]

References

(1)   Eiche, J. E. "What's a Synthesizer: Simple Answers to Common Questions about the Musical Technology". Leonard Books: Milwaukee, **1987.**

(2)   Schrader, B. "Introduction to Electro-Acoustic Music". Prentice Hall: Englewood Cliffs, **1982.**

(3)   Horn, D. T. "Digital Electronic Music Synthesizers". Tab Books: Blue Ridge Summit, PA, **1988.**

(4)   Charbeneau, T. <u>Futurist.</u> **1987** 21(5),35–7.

(5)   Mathews, M. V.; Pierce, J. R. <u>Sci. Amer.</u> **1987** 256(2),126–33.

(6)   Thompson, T. <u>Bus. Wk.</u> **1987** (40),114–16.

Part Five

A Variety of Projects That Incorporate Research

Chapter 17

An Analysis of a Single Work of Literature

This chapter introduces you to two assignments that you may be asked to write about literature:

- analyzing one work of literature, based solely upon your experience of reading and rereading

- incorporating the ideas of critics into your analysis of one work of literature.

You can adapt the methods you use for these assignments for writing about other arts such as film, music, painting, dance, and architecture.

Analyzing a Work of Literature Based upon Your Observations

Within studies of literature, assignments vary widely depending upon the priorities of teachers. You may be asked to concentrate on the characters, or the ideas, or the use of language, or the form of the work at hand. Each of these approaches requires specific instructions and terminology.

Nevertheless, certain methods and standards apply to nearly all assignments. They all require that your assertions be supported by *evidence*, and in literary essays, evidence means specific quotations and details from the literature itself—anything that another person could observe readily when you point it out. Whether or not a phrase is "sad" or "well written" is not directly observable, but any reader can observe that a phrase is "brief" or that two words in it "rhyme" or that a character "repeats" a phrase. So your job as a reader is to observe well, and as a writer it is to tie your feelings about the literature to the concrete details that gave you those feelings.

An Example

You can practice relating observable facts to feelings and ideas with the title and two opening lines of a poem by Langston Hughes, "Mother to Son":

> Well, son, I'll tell you,
> Life for me ain't been no crystal stair.

On the level of observations you might note that the title refers to a mother and a son. The first line uses "son" in direct address. You might note the use of "ain't" and the double negative ("ain't . . . no"). You might note the use of "I" and "you." And you might note the comparison of life to a "crystal stair."

From these observations, you can form ideas about the poem: about who is speaking and about the person she is speaking to. You might also form ideas about a contrast between "ain't . . . no" and a "crystal stair." These ideas could be about how poetic language works, or they could be about differences between social groups, or both.

When you write about a poem or other work of literature, you should present the ideas you have come to, and you should support your ideas with observable facts. You might say, for instance,

> In the opening lines of Langston Hughes's "Mother to Son," the
>
> mother expresses the contrast between her life and a "crystal stair." The lan-
>
> guage and the image that she uses make the contrast clear and strong: we
>
> associate "crystal" with wealth, comfort, and beautiful light. A "crystal stair"
>
> would be expensive and fragile. But the speaker says that her life has not
>
> been that way, and her language—"ain't been no"—suggests that she is a
>
> working-class woman.

A reader might disagree with some of the ideas in this paragraph, but the writer has made clear where within the poem those ideas come from, and to disagree effectively, the reader would need to show how other conclusions can be drawn from the same lines.

Preparing Your Paper

When you are given a text to read and to analyze, you can best approach the assignment in several steps:

First, carefully read the text—the work of literature you are studying. Make sure that you understand the sequence of events. Take note of your first impressions. Your first reading should be a time to enjoy the text, to respond without the pressure to come up with answers or ideas.

Next, freewrite about the topic, if your teacher has given you one, or otherwise about the thoughts and feelings the reading led you to. Get down your initial responses. A good idea—especially when reading a long novel or a series of shorter works—is to keep a reading journal. Whenever your reading leads you into a line of thought, note the number of the page you are on and take a few minutes to write down your thoughts. Later you can search through your journal for your best ideas, and you can also use your journal to find the parts of the text that you responded to most strongly.

Formulate your ideas and reread the text. Review the assignment you have been given; reread your freewriting; then write out several ideas about the assignment that you might stress in an essay. At this point don't reject any ideas—your purpose is to collect and articulate several possibilities. Then reread the text (the work of literature) itself, searching for evidence that supports your ideas and for evidence that changes your ideas. Decide which ideas you feel most committed to and most able to back up.

Make a plan which does more than recount the story. In a literature essay, you should not slip into merely repeating what the text says ("This happened . . . then this . . . then this . . . "). Instead, make a list of the main points you would like to establish. Under each point, list the evidence or examples that will best demonstrate it. Your goal is to show how your ideas are supported by the text.

For instance, if you are studying *Oedipus the King* by Sophocles, do not begin by saying that that there was a plague in Thebes, then that Oedipus heard from an oracle, and so forth. Instead, you need to highlight your own ideas. You may be most interested in the way Oedipus changes during the play. You could make one part of your paper establish that he is domineering early in the play, using evidence that supports that opinion, and make the second part of your paper establish that he is more responsive to others in the play's last scene. The point is that your essay should be organized one idea of your own at a time—not one event in the story at a time.

As you write, present your evidence. Remember that your job as a writer about literature is to identify the details in the text that support your ideas. You need to make clear any abstract words that you rely on ("vivid," "descriptive," "tragic," "evil," and so forth). Explain what you mean and use examples and brief quotations, being sure to say why they demonstrate your ideas ("We know that the speaker in "Mother to Son" is a mother from the title and from the use of direct address in the first line—'Well, son, . . .' "). For detailed information on the use of quotations, see chapter 11.

At the end of your essay, you should be able to stress some general ideas that the reader will understand because he or she has looked carefully, with you as the guide, at the details of the text.

Pitfalls to Watch for

- Too much plot summary

- Too many abstract ideas and vague terms—not enough concrete examples and quotations

- Using very long quotations instead of a number of brief ones

- Not making clear why you used a quotation

Conventions of Literary Essays:

Your Title   You must make up your own title, not merely use the title of the work. You can incorporate the work's title into your own:

The Vision of Hope in Langston Hughes's "Mother to Son"

Titles of Texts   Underline or italicize titles of books, plays, films, periodicals, and other long works. Place quotation marks around titles of poems, stories, essays, and other short works.

Author's Name   You should use the author's full name the first time you refer to him or her; after that, use only the last name without Ms. or Mr.

Identifying Author and Title   Early in your essay, state the author and title of the work you are analyzing. Take care of *commas* by using one of these patterns to begin:

"Mother to Son," by Langston Hughes . . . .

In "Mother to Son," Langston Hughes . . . .

Langston Hughes's "Mother to Son" . . . .

Langston Hughes, in "Mother to Son," . . . .

Verb Tenses   Stay in the present tense—the most graceful tense for referring to a poem or story. Even though the story uses past tense ("She slid
down the bannister with great éclat") you should use present tense:

Elvira shows her wildness when she slides down Mr. Harrington's bannister.

If you try to use past tense, you will find yourself slipping into the present
tense.

Quoting Poetry   When you quote more than one line of poetry, skip a
line and set off the whole quotation 10 spaces from the left margin. The
point is to reproduce the same line ending that the poet used:

Well, son, I'll tell you,

Life for me ain't been no crystal stair.

(If the poet's line won't fit on your line, indent the rest of it an extra five
spaces.)

Bibliographical Information   At the end of the paper give the edition of
the text that you have used: author, title of poem or short story (if applicable), title of book, editor or translator (if applicable), city of publication,
publisher, date of this edition, and page(s) of poem or story (if applicable):

Langston Hughes. "Mother to Son." Selected Poems of Langston

Hughes. New York: Knopf, 1970, p. 187.

If the book was originally published in an edition different from yours, put
the original date of publication after the title:

Kate Chopin. The Awakening. 1899. New York: Avon, 1972.

For bibliographical format, see chapter 15. Note that when only one source
is listed, the author is identified first name first.

Page References   In your paper, indicate the source of each quotation by
putting the page number in parentheses following the quotation. (See chap-

ter 14 on parenthetical citations.) For a poem, give the line number; for the Bible, give chapter and verse; for a play, give act and scene (and line number, if listed).

The first chapter of Hawthorne's The Scarlet Letter puns on the mix of church

and state in the "steeple-crowned hats" of the Puritans (35).

"Life for me ain't been no crystal stair" (2).

"There shall be weeping and gnashing of teeth" (Luke 14:28).

In The Winter's Tale, Shakespeare includes a beautiful catalog of the "flow'rs

o' th' spring" (4.4.113).

Incorporating the Ideas of Critics

Most often in literature classes, you will be asked to write papers which give your own responses and observations about different works of literature. However, at times you might be assigned a research paper in conjunction with a work of literature you have read. In this case, you will usually be asked to read critical material which offers interpretation and analysis of the work. In this kind of assignment, you should take the same approach recommended in this book for other research papers: Start with your own point of view and then find evidence through your research to support and develop that point of view.

The term *primary text* refers to the work you are studying. For example, if you were doing a study of Ursula K. LeGuin's collection of short stories, *Orisinian Tales*, the entire book would be the primary text. If you were studying only one short story from the collection, for example "A Week in the Country," only the short story would be considered the primary text. *Secondary sources*, on the other hand, are the critical studies you read—articles and books *about* the literature.

Read the Primary Text Carefully

Before you can read critics with intelligence and judgment, you must patiently read and think over the primary text, the work of literature, that you and the critics are responding to. Freewrite at length to explore your own responses to the details of the text. You can evaluate critics and write a sensible essay only if you have formulated your own impressions of the literature itself.

Choose Critics to Study

First learn the basics—the writer's biography and major works—by reading one or more of the following:

- the introductions to editions of the book you are studying
- encyclopedias
- *The Oxford Companion to American Literature* (or to *English* or to other literatures)

These sources often will identify the best-known critical studies of your text. You should also consult your teacher, who may know the best critics to read. You can also consult bibliographies:

- *The Norton Anthology of English Literature* (or of *American* or *World Literature*) and similar anthologies have selected bibliographies for many writers.
- *The MLA Bibliography,* in bound volumes for each year and on computer, lists all articles and books about literature published that year.
- Recent articles in scholarly journals (listed in the *MLA Bibliography*) will cite important books and articles in the *Works Cited* pages at the end of each article.

By using these sources, you will find that several major studies are cited repeatedly by a number of sources. These are the ones to read, along with a few recent articles, for an overview of major criticism. Be sure to read at least four critics for a balanced sampling.

Read the Critics Carefully and Critically

Take notes on their main ideas. If you are reading just one chapter, take time to read the preface and introduction to understand the critic's approach and emphasis.

Look for ideas that seem true to you. "True" here means close to your experience of the work. Be open to reconsidering your first impressions, even changing them completely, but also remember that your experience as a reader has value and must be the heart of your essay.

Don't be too intimidated by the critics. You can learn from critics while still recognizing that they have their own preferences and biases. Use the following questions to assess each critic's approach:

- Is the critic mainly responding to other critics?

- Is the critic mainly interested in a philosophical or historical point?

- Is the critic putting the work in the context of the author's life, the historical period, or the works of other writers?

- Is the critic concerned with the work's style and form (use of language, patterns of images, the order of the parts)?

- Is the critic examining and elucidating specific passages (quotations) in detail?

- Does the critic write clearly? Does the critic speak, as an experienced and caring person, about issues that matter?

Write Your Essay

After you have finished reading the critics and taking notes, *freewrite* again, without notes. What is your assignment? Answer it as directly as possible. What is clear and important to you? What is your evidence? (Which examples will you stress? Which specific passages will you examine in detail?)

Depending on your assignment, incorporate the ideas of critics. If you have been asked to write a *review of the criticism* in the field, you may want to use one of the following plans:

- chronology—early critics first, then recent ones

- comparison—two or three typical approaches

- comparison—two or three of the most valuable critics

More likely, you have been asked to *develop your own ideas, incorporating critics*. In this case, try one of the following plans:

- Present your own ideas in a logical sequence of paragraphs. Along the way, give credit to ideas from critics by mentioning their names or quoting them briefly (using the proper form of documentation—see chapters 14–15). Do not cover one critic at a time, but refer to various critics as their points relate to your main points. Be sure the critic's idea fits into the point of *your* paragraph.

- Argue against a critic—one who is well known, to whom others refer. Begin by explaining as fairly as possible the critic's idea, quoting a key passage or two. Be as sure as you can that you are not misrepresenting the critic. Then present your counter-arguments point by point. (Give credit to any other critics whose ideas you use in refuting the idea of the first critic. See chapters 14–15 for the proper form of documentation to use.)

In writing about critics, you need to balance two priorities:

- Independent thinking—not admiring everything you read but trusting your own sense of what is true

- Respect for other writers—not referring to them on a first name basis, not blithely making fun of their ideas, and not hastily jumping to conclusions about what they are saying

As always, conclude by stressing what you found most important in your study of the work at hand.

For an annotated example of a student essay that analyzes a work of literature and incorporates the ideas of critics, see the appendix, page 189.

Chapter
18

A Study of a Social Issue

In many courses—sociology, economics, political science, English—research projects often concentrate on social issues. Almost any subject you choose to study has inherent in it some problem which affects society. It's easy to see social issues in topics such as the environment, health care, education, or politics. But even less obvious topics such as sports, nutrition, and entertainment contain within them social issues. For example, in sports, you might investigate the challenge professional baseball has faced in bringing together players from diverse ethnic groups. In nutrition, you might make a study of the lack of nutrition in hospital food. In entertainment, you might look at the sex-role stereotyping in Saturday morning cartoons.

Any time you have to write about a social issue, you need to have a very strong feeling and point of view about the problem you choose. Your strong concern about the problem is what will motivate you to study it thoroughly and to seek solutions.

In a social problem paper, you

- Describe a major problem in your field of interest—a problem that affects many other people
- Demonstrate why you consider this problem serious; back up your position with information gathered through research
- Explain some of the solutions that authorities in the field think are possible
- Explain your own ideas of the best possible solution

Preliminary Planning

You may already have a social problem in mind that you want to write about, something that has bothered you for a long time. If not, take 30 minutes for some brainstorming and freewriting. Chapter 2 explains in detail how to search for a topic you care about. Look for a problem that affects others as well as yourself and that has some potential solutions.

Here are some examples of how students took a personal interest or problem and chose a social issue related to it:

Personal Interest/Problem	Social Issue
Overeating	How people eat to satisfy emotional needs
Becoming a professional dancer	How dancers jeopardize their physical and emotional health
Insomnia	Overuse of sleeping pills

Here are some social problems that other students felt passionate about enough to want to study them:

- The inhumane treatment of incarcerated juvenile criminals

- Why solar energy has failed

- The continuing job discrimination against black men

- The devastating effect of fish farming on our environment

These examples may give you some ideas for finding a problem that you feel strongly about.

When you have chosen your problem, be sure that you have defined it in a narrow enough way that you can do a thorough job.

Finally, take a few minutes to freewrite about your own personal perspective on the issue.

Conducting Your Research

A study of a social issue affords you the opportunity to use a wide variety of sources of information. Suppose that you are taking the stand that hospital food is poor in nutrition. Some possible sources include:

Newspapers and magazines

Books, both popular and scholarly

Interviews with experts

Surveys or questionnaires—published ones or your own

Television and radio programs

See chapters 4, 6, and 8 for more ideas for sources.

In considering which sources to explore, try to include sources that represent different perspectives. Besides reading up on nutrition, for example, you would want to talk with hospital nutritionists to understand their perspectives.

Writing the Paper

Here's a suggested plan for how you might go about presenting your paper. There are two attitudes you might adopt, depending on your feelings. You may have found several legitimate points of view and want to present a balanced comparison. On the other hand, you may have discovered that one position is right and another wrong. In this case, your goal is to argue effectively for your point of view.

Introduction

The thrust of the introduction is to show that there really is a serious problem. You might begin with startling statistics or with a brief anecdote that will engage your reader's concern. Whatever opening you choose, make it emphatic. Chris McDonnell, a student writing about the damaging effects on the environment of fish farming, began:

> The rapid development of fish farming has created a new source of danger on our planet. One reason for this danger is the pollution produced by the farms: one salmon cage, with 30,000 salmon crammed into 50 square feet, pours out raw sewage equivalent to the untreated sewage of 10,000 people (MacBride 26). Can you imagine the effects of this waste on the surroundings? And this is only the beginning.
>
> MacBride, Laurie. "Alliance Fights for Georgia Strait." <u>Canadian Dimension</u> Oct. 1990: 24–27.

Background Information

What will your reader need to know in order to see the problem and follow your analysis of it? You may need to give a brief history of the problem (for example, the recent rise of salmon farming in the United States), and you may need to explain certain technicalities (how a salmon farm works).

Discussion of Problem

The main part of your paper should give several points of view from your different sources. Use very specific information—facts and quotations—to show the causes of the problem and the effects of this problem on people and society. Be sure to weave several sources together:

> In various parts of the world, fish hatcheries are allowing some of their fish to escape and to spread disease to wild fish. Laurie MacBride describes "new parasites and diseases" (26) occurring in the Georgia Bay of Ontario. Stephen Cline describes a similar problem "traced to a hatchery" (36) in Norway. The problem is further aggravated, as Marcia Barinaga points out, because antibiotics used in hatcheries eventually "promote the growth of antibiotic-resistant bacteria" in the ocean (630).

> Barinaga, Marcia. "Fish, Money, and Science in Puget Sound." *News and Comment*. 9 Feb. 1990: 631.

> Cline, Stephen. "Down on the Fish Farm." *Sierra* Mar.-Apr. 1989: 34–38.

> MacBride, Laurie. "Alliance Fights for Georgia Strait." *Canadian Dimension* Oct. 1990: 24–27.

Presentation of Your Experience

If the problem has had an impact on you or if your research has intensified your sense of the problem, this is a good point at which to present your own case. Chris McDonnell wrote:

> In 1988 I witnessed the drastic effects that fish farms have on the environment. The bays around my home in Ireland were polluted with fish wastes and chemicals which killed thousands of lobsters and other shellfish.

> Don't, however, let personal experiences take over the paper; instead make them serve as one form of evidence that you are offering.

Presentation of Possible Solutions

Lay out the best solutions you have found for the problem, including the ideas of experts along with any of your own. Evaluate the extent to which each solution might work. You can distinguish small-scale local solutions from global solutions that would be ideal. For example, in the study of fish farms, Chris McDonnell distinguishes between what individual fish farmers can do and what the federal government can do.

Conclusion

End with a strong statement. Either tell the impact of your research on you or stress the most important point that you have learned. For example, Chris McDonnell concluded:

I would not be opposed to an increase in aqua culture if pollution were decreased to a reasonable level. Aqua culture could be a great and successful industry. But we must prevent pollution of the environment or we, like some fish farms, will self-destruct.

For an example of a complete paper about a social issue—the overuse of sleeping pills—see the appendix, page 207.

Chapter
19

A Report on a Scientific or Technological Subject

Scientific Research

The scientific approach applies not only to laboratory sciences, but to the social sciences as well. In fact, you can apply the scientific method to any aspect of learning.

When you think of scientific research, you probably think first and foremost of experiments. But professional scientists know that experimentation—while it is the heart of research—is not the only method they need to use. In fact, there are three layers of scientific research: *reviewing the literature, networking,* and *experimentation.*

Reviewing the Literature

The first part of thorough scientific research—and perhaps the only part you need for a particular assignment—is library work. Before scientists can design an experiment or even define their goals, they need to catch up on what is known.

If you are given a scientific problem or topic to investigate, your first step is to find several broad review articles. A review article is a summary of research in a specific field. For many projects, review articles will suffice; for more advanced research, they are the best starting place. You can begin with a specialized encyclopedia, like *The McGraw-Hill Encyclopedia of Science and Technology* or the *Kirk-Othmer Encyclopedia of Chemical Technology*—or even a regular encyclopedia. But for more up-to-date and specialized review articles, you will need to look into scientific journals. Begin with the bound volumes of a periodical index such as *Biological Abstracts* or *Index Medicus.* (See the appendix for a fuller listing.) The advantage of bound copies over the computerized listings of the same sources is that you can browse, look over neighboring categories, and get an overview of where your topic fits in. Look through one or two recent volumes, noting any articles marked "Review" or "R."

At this point, a computer search using a database specific to science and technology will be most efficient. But you will need to narrow your focus and find key words that will identify your exact subject. Your search through bound volumes will have given you some key words to try. Once you find an article, you can call up, on the database, the headings under which it is listed. You can also call up its bibliography. When you have a few key words, follow directions on the computer or see page 44 for methods of getting just the list you want. The art of choosing a subject heading is to be neither too broad (getting uselessly long lists) nor too narrow (missing useful articles).

Having found a useful list of review articles, you will now want a printed list. Start by asking for the first five only, to see if they are appropriate. Since the list will give the most recent articles first, five may suffice.

Networking

Networking can begin by letting teachers and friends know about your project and asking for leads (see p. 24). Once you know the basics of the topic, you can also contact some experts. You may feel that you have no right to speak to actual researchers in the field you are studying, but in fact most people are happy to help. You can call or visit:

- The author of an article you have read
- The public relations department of a company that produces or supplies a particular product
- Government-funded laboratories and other research facilities (Centers for Disease Control and Prevention, wildlife preserves, and so on)
- Government granting agencies and private foundations (National Institutes of Health, Carnegie Foundation, and so forth)
- The science departments or the technology transfer office of a major university
- Museums of natural history or of science and technology (the staff, the displays, and the libraries)

Government granting agencies often can give you an overview of current research since they know who is doing what right now. Businesses often can send you brochures and samples. In any interview, however brief, let the person know that you are a beginner and ask for leads to other sources. (See chapter 8 for advice on conducting interviews.)

Experimentation

Ultimately, the basis of all scientific research is hands-on experimentation. If you are experimenting independently, you will need to consult professors or other experts in your field to learn how best to design and conduct a specific experiment. As a preparation for writing, your best method is to keep copious notes, not only during the experiment but before it (as you meet with professors and plan your experiment) and afterward (as you analyze data and draw conclusions). Write down in a notebook what you are trying and how you will try it. Make careful observations and record them (including dates, names and telephone numbers of people you consult, and so forth. Keeping a notebook and proceeding systematically are essential to the success of the project.

Scientific Writing

Whether you are doing a library research paper or you are writing up an experiment, you must adjust your style for your reader's needs. You might be doing a term paper for an English teacher in a composition course, or you might be writing on the same topic for a teacher of physical chemistry. Your anticipated reader will determine how much technical terminology you use and how much you have to explain.

Reporting an Experiment

The report of an experiment usually has five parts:

Introduction: a summary of previous studies and an explanation of why you are conducting this research

Methodology: an explanation of exactly what you did, in such detail that a reader could reproduce the experiment

Results: data, tables, charts, observations, and an analysis of the results

Conclusions

References (See pp. 145–148)

In writing up an experiment, use the passive voice. The convention among scientists is to write, "10 g of NaCl was stirred into the solution," rather than "We stirred 10 g of NaCl into the solution."

Reports of Library Research

Writing a report of library research in science or technology is not very different from writing any report of library research. Therefore you should rely on parts III and IV of this book for basic instructions. As in all writing, remember that you are guiding someone through what you have found out.

You may be asked to add an *abstract* (see p. 70); you may need to use *charts or illustrations* (see chapter 20); and, depending on your reader's expertise, you may need to add a *glossary* (an alphabetical list of technical terms you have used, with their definitions). Finally, for reports in science, depending on your professor's preference, you may need to use the ACS (American Chemical Society) system of documentation explained on pages 145–148.

The final assembly of your report should be in the following order:

Title page

Abstract (if required)

Outline or table of contents

The paper (either including charts or illustrations in context or supplying them after the references)

References

Glossary (if needed)

Appendix (if needed)

Chapter 20

An Illustrated Report

Illustrations can communicate a large amount of information in a small space. We take for granted how much we depend on illustrations in our daily reading, yet most college papers do not use them. In fact, certain topics cannot be covered adequately without illustrations—for instance, topics in the visual arts or process reports. Illustrations can be charts, graphs, drawings, diagrams, or photographs. You can create them yourself or photocopy them from other sources.

This chapter presents two approaches to illustration:

- You can insert a few key illustrations into a report.
- You can make illustrations the central focus and create an illustrated booklet.

Using Illustrations as Part of Your Paper

In the process of planning a research paper, you might decide that it can be enhanced by adding visuals. For example, if you are writing a paper about how essential new housing for senior citizens will become in the next few years, you might want to add a graph showing how the population over 70 years of age has increased during the past 20 years. Or if you are writing a paper on the use of animals in cosmetic testing, you might include a photo showing the effect of the Draize eye irritancy test on rabbits. If you're writing a paper about the presidency of Theodore Roosevelt, you might use a political cartoon from the period. Even one or two well-selected visuals can add substance and interest to your paper. During your research, if you come across interesting illustrations, make clear photocopies of them for possible use, being certain to write down all the bibliographical information on each one of them.

In addition to using copies of illustrations from other sources, you can also create your own by taking photographs, making drawings, or creating computer graphics. Computers have made graphics fun and easy to use. For many illustrations, you must use a graphics software program. However, most computers now have some built-in graphic possibilities—enough so that you can create simple charts and bar graphs.

Here are a few guidelines for incorporating visuals into the text of your paper:

- First be certain that the illustration gives *additional* information or *clarifies* a statement in the text. Don't just stick in a visual for effect. It has to have a purpose.

- Keep it simple. Each visual should communicate a single message.

- Be sure that it is large enough to be clearly seen. Enlarge it if you need to.

- Be sure that you have a good, sharp copy of your illustration. Often a photocopy is clearer than the original.

- Place the visuals into the text right at the points at which you have discussed them; however, if the visuals will be too disruptive to the paper, add them in an appendix at the end.

- Secure illustrations into your paper with double-stick tape or glue on the back—rather than taping the edges—for a neater look.

- Give the visual a commentary so that the reader clearly understands why you've included it.

- If your illustration is not original, give the source of the illustration, including page number, immediately after the commentary. Include the source in your *Works Cited* as well. If you are using an original photograph, identify the photographer, location, and date; if you use original drawings, make clear that they are your own.

Creating an Illustrated Booklet

If your topic is one that is built around illustrations start to finish, you can create an illustrated booklet. In this case, the illustrations will determine the text of your paper. Some typical subjects which lend themselves naturally to an illustrated booklet include:

photography

art and art history

architecture

advertising

 industrial design

instructions—how to . . .

If you can write your paper without needing illustrations, you have no real reason to do an illustrated booklet. Your topic should be one which *has* to have visuals in order to be clearly understood.

One format for this project that you've probably seen is the photographic essay in popular magazines. Before you put your own illustrated booklet together, you might look at *Vanity Fair, National Geographic,* or *Life* for ideas and layout.

Here are some guidelines to help you create a professional-looking illustrated booklet.

Narrow Down Your Topic

Before beginning, you must take time to narrow down your idea. You'll want to come up with a specific, narrow focus. Instead of using "Advertising of Alcohol in Magazines," you would do better to narrow down to "The Use of Sports to Sell Alcohol."

Here are some other examples of specific topics that would lend themselves to an illustrated booklet:

Matisse's Paper Collages

The Construction of the Empire State Building

The Technology of 12th Century Cathedral Windows

The Training of a Guide Dog

Techniques for Photographing House Fires

The Making of a Pinball Machine

Narrowing your topic will also save you time in searching for illustrations.

Find the Illustrations

Allow plenty of time over several days to search for or create your illustrations. They will be the heart of your essay, so give them real attention. You'll need to gather many more than you'll actually use. If you are using published illustrations, don't depend on only one or two sources. In the library, you can search in databases to find visuals by typing in your subject plus one of the following headings: "Illustrations," "Pictorial works," "Caricatures and cartoons," and "Descriptions." Besides the library, consider using some of the sources discussed in chapter 4.

Make sure that your illustrations are clean and easy to see. Make enlargements if necessary. You might occasionally want to include color photocopies of important illustrations.

Also, be certain to write down all the bibliographical information on each published illustration because you'll need to give the exact source for each one.

Plan Your Illustrated Booklet

Once you've located all your illustrations, spread them out on a table and play around with the order of them. Look for a sequence of illustrations that will tell a story or build to a point.

Write a rough draft of what you want to say. This will become the text of your booklet. After you write your text, you may find you want to rearrange your illustrations.

Decide on Your Layout

Layout—the arrangement of text and illustrations—is the artistic part of your project.

- Decide which illustrations need a full page and which need to go together. Most of the time, one illustration per page is very effective; however, sometimes you will want the reader to compare two or more illustrations.

- Decide which illustrations need to be enlarged, reduced, or cropped. A full-page magazine photograph will have to be smaller to allow marginal white space and room for commentary. Reduce it if you want the whole picture, or crop out one part.

- Decide on the balance of commentary and illustration for each page.

- Leave plenty of white space. Don't crowd the pages.

Give Each Illustration a Commentary

All the illustrations must be held together with "connective tissue." Write a complete commentary for each illustration. The commentary must say something significant about each illustration. Most of the commentaries should be several sentences or a paragraph. The commentaries themselves should read smoothly from one to the other; they are the body of your text.

Do Not Include Any Illustration Which Does Not Have Explanatory Text

Don't add any tagged-on or extra illustrations just for the sake of filling up space. Each chosen illustration must be justified with an important statement that makes a concrete point. Ask yourself: "Why am I including this in the essay? What does it show?" If you don't have an answer, leave it out.

Write an Introduction and a Conclusion

In addition to the illustrations with their text, you must add a significant introduction of several paragraphs and a conclusion of several paragraphs. Your introduction and conclusion should frame the essay and give it further meaning. The introduction should "set up" the booklet by giving necessary information before you present the illustrations; the conclusion should make a final statement and tie the essay together in a meaningful way.

Acknowledge Your Sources

Give the source for each illustration in parentheses at the bottom of the illustration. For an unpublished illustration, use a simple byline (by Louise Crowe); for an illustration from a published source, include the author's last name and the page number where you found it. Add a *Works Cited* page at the end of your paper (See chapters 14 and 15). For original illustrations, include the name of the artist in parentheses: (by Louise Goldberg).

Assemble Your Booklet

Take time to make your booklet attractive and durable:

- Use heavy paper.

- Use glue stick, double stick tape, or rubber cement to attach illustrations. Consider photocopying the final paste-up so that illustrations don't come loose.

- Type all text and commentary.

- Add attractive covers which might incorporate some of your illustrations and bind the booklet together in a substantial way.

Chapter 21

A Report of an Interview

The interviews you may be most familiar with are probably the profiles in popular magazines. Such interviews concentrate on personalities and feature information about the person's appearance, opinions, home decor, or private life. However, reports of interviews in college courses will be more likely to concentrate on *information* learned in an interview. The topic rather than the personality will dominate. For a report of this kind, you should choose a topic for which books and articles would not provide inside or up-to-date information. You can use interviews to gain:

- a behind-the-scenes view of the field
- an in-depth account of one aspect of a subject
- the ideas of an expert who has not published those ideas
- the testimony of a participant in an historic event
- current developments or experiments in the field

Remember that this kind of informational interview is not a record of someone's personal history. The primary purpose of such an interview is to obtain information you would not normally be able to get elsewhere—or at least to get a new slant on some particular topic. Your report should reflect this emphasis on information.

Before You Begin

If you haven't already conducted the interview, arrange for one now. See chapter 8, "Conducting an Interview," for suggestions.

- Go over all your notes from the interview and listen to the tape if you made one.

- Study all the direct quotations you took down and see if you can find a common idea, or recurrent theme, among them. If so, group quotations together accordingly.

- Write out a couple of paragraphs about how the interview affected your own thinking and attitudes. What was the most valuable aspect of the interview for you?

Writing the Paper

Avoid a question-and-answer format. Although some magazines use this kind of organization, it leaves little room for pulling the information together into a central focus. Neither should you merely recount the interview in the order in which it occurred.

Here is a better way to organize your paper so that you end up with a report that is complete both in information and in your responses:

- In your introduction, give the name and position of the person you interviewed and the date and location of the interview. Next, state the major information you hoped to obtain—in other words, the topic you went to the interview with.

- Then in several paragraphs explain specifically what you learned about this topic from the interview. This is the main part of your paper, so develop it fully. When necessary, make clear the questions you asked. Be sure that you are giving a fair representation of the person's views.

- Include short, direct quotations from your interviewee. Keep these brief, make them as accurate as possible, and punctuate them with quotation marks. In addition, you should summarize and paraphrase some of the conversation and add your own comments to it.

- If you followed the suggestions for conducting an interview in chapter 8 and you asked the interviewee about a major problem in the field, use the last part of your paper to explain this problem. Then discuss in detail all the solutions, if any, the person thinks are possible.

- End with your own opinions and assessments of the information you obtained. Be certain to explain what you found out that was totally new information for you or what you learned that changed your thinking in any way.

- Attach a list of the questions you asked—in the order you asked them.

A final note: If, during the process of writing your paper, you are unclear about some information or specific quotations, call your interviewee and ask for clarification.

Chapter 22

An Essay Based upon Family History

Your own family can lead you to a variety of research projects that, because they pertain to your family, have particular personal value for you. You can construct a family tree, or record a story that has been repeated in the family, or tell the life story of a grandparent. All of these projects begin by recalling what you've heard and then talking with your relatives. You might start with your mother or father, but then need to call an aunt in Montana to fill in details. Later, you might go to the library to corroborate facts (the date of a hurricane, for instance) or to learn about the larger events surrounding your family's story (perhaps the migration of African-American families from the rural South to the urban North).

By exploring your family's story, you will learn about your own past, your heritage; at the same time, you may get to know your relatives in a new way.

Exploring the Life of an Older Relative

Choose a living older relative whose life intrigues you—perhaps a grandparent, aunt or uncle, or parent—someone from a generation before yours. He or she may have come to America from another country or may have overcome a serious hardship or may simply have led what seems to you to be an interesting life. Remember, however, that every life is interesting and has its drama. Grand, historic events are not the only dramatic ones: The story of your aunt working in an airplane factory during World War II may turn out to be as intriguing to you as the story of her husband away at war.

Before you sit down to talk with your relative, you should freewrite about what you already know about this person's life or make a list of incidents that you have heard about. You may be interested in his or her whole story or concentrate on one part of the story. End by listing the questions you wonder about—questions you want to ask your relative. Take time with this list; write down at least ten questions, and think them over, so that you will ask what you really want to know.

Interviewing Your Relative

Now you are ready to schedule a time when you can ask your questions and listen to your relative's story. As in any interview, you want the person to feel at ease and to get into a relaxed flow of conversation. You want the conversation to follow its own path, perhaps leading to unexpected topics. But you'll have to overcome the odd formality of the situation. Here are some tips:

Tell the relative why you are doing this interview. If it is a school assignment, let him or her know that you need help.

Choose a time and place where you won't be interrupted. Allow at least 90 minutes—more time than you think you will need. Don't get caught short of time; the conversation is likely to get interesting, likely to ramble into unexpected stories that you will be glad to hear.

Use a tape recorder. Ask if it's okay to use one. Put it close enough so that your relative's voice will record clearly. The initial awkwardness will pass quickly, and you'll have a tape to refer to as you prepare your paper—and one that you may want to keep.

Start with easy questions. What is our family tree—which relatives do *you* remember? What was the house like where you were a child? Who else was there? What was the neighborhood like? What did you play? How did you meet _____ (your husband or wife)? Ask about "family stories" you have heard—get your relative's versions of these stories.

Listen for seemingly "minor" details. Your relative may think that the details of his or her past are of no interest and may say, "You don't want to know about all of that, do you?" And you, too, may not suspect how much that you will value can come out of the seemingly minor details of what people ate and how they cooked or what they did for a good time. But you never know which tiny detail will remind your relative of a really interesting story. So say that you *do* want to know the details, and ask about daily life—not just about the events that get into history books.

Ask questions in a way that lets your relative expand—avoid "yes"/"no" questions. To ask, "Did you have turkey for Thanksgiving?" will not lead as far as to ask, "What all was on the table that Thanksgiving Day?"

Allow for silent time. Use your list of questions whenever your relative loses momentum, but in general let his or her memory guide the conversation. Silence is okay—jumping in with a new question too soon might cut off an important thought.

Make the interview an enjoyable conversation for both of you. Remember that your relative is doing you a favor and that the best way to show gratitude is to welcome the thoughts and stories that come up. (For more tips on interviewing, see chapter 8.)

Writing an Essay Based upon Your Interview

At this point, you can write a paper reflecting upon one aspect of your interview.

A Reflective Essay One excellent approach is to write down one story— one event—in full detail and to add your own reflections to it. Why is this story important to your relative? What does it mean to you at this point in your own life? What general knowledge does the story lead you to?

A Comparison between Generations A second approach is to make a very specific comparison between "then" and "now." Possibilities include:

- a typical "night out"
- doctoring then and now
- the choices your grandmother had compared with those of women today
- two wars: the feelings of veterans
- elementary school (maybe comparing your grandparent's schooling not only with yours, but also with your nephew's or niece's or child's schooling)

In writing this comparison, you should tell all about one time—either then or now—before telling all about the other. Conclude by going into the difference that the change over time makes.

These topics could lead you to talk with a second relative or could send you back to the first relative for more details.

Using Research to Explore One Aspect of Your Relative's Story

Where you go from here—what further research and writing you do— depends upon what interested you in your interview. After your interview,

you need to see what you've got. Write down what you learned that surprised you or that made the biggest impression. Write how you felt about
the interview.

Here are two directions in which you might proceed to further explore family history:

Choosing a Subject for Further Research

Place your relative's story in the context of a historical event.   Find
out how typical your relative's experience was. Again, you will need to
choose one part of his or her story. Some possibilities include:

- immigration
- life during the Depression
- war (overseas; on the home front; the return of veterans)
- protest movements; racial or ethnic conflicts
- migrations (country to city; city to suburbs)
- catastrophes (a hurricane, an epidemic, a shortage)

"Oral history" is one way to compare your relative's story with the experiences of others. If you enjoyed the interview, you might find other people
to interview—neighbors or friends of your relative or of your classmates. In
oral history, you compile the memories of a number of people, searching for
common themes. Each interview will lead you to revise your list of questions as you gradually clarify your focus.

The library is essential to finding out how typical your relative's story is.
Encyclopedias and general American histories can give you background information about the event or time period in question. Newspapers and magazines from that time will give you rich and particular information. Another
possibility is to find memoirs, diaries, and letters by people who lived
through the same events. See chapter 6 and consult the librarian for help
with finding these sources.

Pursue one specific topic that your relative discussed.   Sometimes a
small part of the story catches your interest. In this case, you might leave
your relative's experience behind for a while and explore a topic the interview has led you to. Maybe your grandfather was a fisherman off the coast
of New Brunswick around 1900, and you would like to know more about
the fishing methods of that time. Maybe your uncle spent time in a sanito-
rium for tuberculosis, and you want to find out about such places. Maybe

your aunt grew up in Coney Island, and you would like to know about that resort in its heyday. For such topics, the right local library might have the best sources—local newspapers, official records, donated collections of memorabilia—and the local librarian or someone at the local historical society might become your best guide.

Writing about Your Research

As in any research project, keep a notebook and freewrite frequently at several points along the way. The shape of the paper you write will depend upon the focus you choose. In any case, no matter which kind of family history you write, you can begin with your relative's experience and keep his or her story as a thread throughout the paper. You should also:

- weave together information from several sources
- decide where to tell background information and how much to tell
- decide what to stress and what to leave out
- include a number of short direct quotations which capture your relative's individuality

At the end, out of all that you have learned, say what is most important to you.

Chapter 23

Taking a Single Topic All the Way Home: An Extended Research Project

At some point in college, you may have the opportunity to undertake a long-term research project—perhaps as a thesis in your major, or as an independent study program, or as an option in a course. An extended project can be one major paper or it can be a series of shorter papers approaching one subject from different angles.

For example, you might be intrigued with the Great Depression in America and want to explore many different aspects of it. In this case, you might read and critique a relevant novel, such as John Steinbeck's *The Grapes of Wrath*; you might investigate the story of your own family during the Depression; you might conduct an interview with a historian about the Depression; you might compile a photographic essay depicting some aspect of the Depression; you could do a paper on a specific government policy during that time.

Doing an extended research project—whether it be one paper or a series of interrelated papers—will take you progressively deeper into your subject and make you an expert in it. The choices are wide open. The main criterion for choosing a subject for an extended research project is that it should be something you feel wholeheartedly committed to and something you can live with for an interval of time.

Directions and advice throughout this book apply to both short and long-term research projects. However, if you are working all term—or all year—on one specialized subject field, there are additional pointers that will help you.

Planning Your Project

It's possible to survive a month-long project on a topic you dislike, but a long-term project requires motivation—best found in selecting a topic you want to spend time with.

- Use the exercises in chapter 2 to find a topic that you really want to study.
- Use chapter 3 to analyze your work style.
- Develop a long-term plan for your project.
- Consult with your instructor and write a research proposal.

The Research Proposal

In writing a research proposal, you will discover whether you are committed to your field of research. Writing it will also help you focus more specifically on the goals, both immediate and long-term, that you hope to meet in conducting your research.

Previewing Your Research

Once you've settled on a topic you feel really energetic about, the next step is to do some library sleuthing.

Do several hours of general reading to gain an overview of the literature available in the field. Consult a recent encyclopedia for a comprehensive summary, and then select a few up-to-date books or articles and browse through them. Look for bibliographies and recommended reading.

Start to compile a *working bibliography*—a list of books and articles on your subject. You will be adding to this as you go along. The purpose of the working bibliography is to be certain that sufficient reference materials are available for your subject. Gather a variety of materials—popular as well as scholarly articles and books, audio-visual sources, interviews, government documents, and so forth. Write down all bibliographical information for each source as well as a brief summary that describes it. These personal summaries will come in handy when you go further into your research. Also, if you are required to turn in an *annotated bibliography* (a bibliography with notations), these summaries can serve as your annotations.

Writing the Proposal

To begin the proposal, give a general introduction to your topic. Write several paragraphs, targeting the material to your reader's level of expertise.

Next add a number of paragraphs in which you justify your choice of topic. Each paragraph should contain one reason, thoroughly explained, as to why you have an interest in this subject. Back up each reason with persuasive evidence. For this section, you might consider your own relationship with the subject in the past, how you are involved with it presently, and how it will figure into your future—and then organize your paper along those lines.

End the paper by stating specifically what you hope to accomplish in your research. Clearly state each of your research goals (there should be several) and briefly explain what steps you plan to take in accomplishing each of them. Add a strong concluding statement that sums up what conducting this research will mean to you.

Attach a *working bibliography* to the end of your proposal to give an overview of the pertinent literature available on the subject. But be selective; include only those sources you have found most helpful so far and expect to use in your research. Also be certain that your sources are not obsolete. Note: Use exactly the same format for a *working bibliography* as you do for a *Works Cited* page (see chapters 15 and 16).

During the Project

Begin writing as soon as you begin reading.   You should not wait to finish your research before you write the paper. This is the biggest difference between writing a long paper and writing a normal term paper. For a term paper, most students do the research, then the writing. But for a thesis or other long paper, you should write parts of the paper as you read, even though you do not know the shape of your final essay and may not use much of what you first write.

Keep a section of your notebook just for notes to yourself.   These notes should be about your sense of the project and where it is leading.

Vary your pace to freshen your thinking.   For example, if you prefer a methodical, regular pace while note-taking or writing, occasionally set a timer for twenty minutes and see how many notes you can take or how many new sources you can find. If you usually operate at breakneck speed, set the timer for thirty minutes, read just a few pages, and then analyze them.

Read a few sources on a contrasting but related topic.   If you are working primarily on a historical topic, check on modern treatment of a parallel topic. For example, look for an article on renovation of the New York subway system in the 1980s to give a fresh perspective on your study of their design in the 1890s. Or balance your study of AIDS with an article on another fatal epidemic—such as cholera, tuberculosis, or polio. Or read an article on the screwball comedy films of the 1930s to contrast with your study of comic elements in Shakespeare. Even if you can't use this new information, reading a different approach will broaden your perspective.

Allow time for collaboration. One problem with long-term projects is that they can be isolating. Find time to discuss your findings with friends and to ask their advice.

Expect to revise a number of times. Put your work into a word processor early. Long papers in particular go through more drafts than you might expect. Revision will entail not only touch-ups but complete changes of emphasis. Allow more time proportionately for revising a long project than you usually do for the revision process.

A Wrap-Up Paper

An optional, final paper in your research project can be an informal paper that sums up the most personally meaningful aspects of your research. This paper gives you a chance to summarize the major information you learned as a result of your research and provides an opportunity for you to evaluate the experience of researching your particular subject. Even if you're not required to write a wrap-up paper, you may well find that writing one is a satisfying experience and that your project director will appreciate reading it.

Before beginning, think back over all the research you've done on this subject and assess what you have actually learned and what impact it has had on you. Think about each of these questions:

- What motivated me to choose this subject?

- What is the most important information I learned?

- Which of my opinions and ideas did this research reinforce or change?

- Do I have any future plans to continue this research or use it in some concrete way?

- Is there any kind of contribution I could make to others now as a result of my new knowledge?

- All in all, what did I gain from doing this project?

Now begin to write your paper in an informal "talking" voice, as if you were telling someone your experience in conducting this research. Give the most important information you gained from the research and evaluate the experience.

If you're stuck for a method to present this paper, here's a basic plan you can follow:

- Begin your paper by introducing the most important information you have learned. Take several paragraphs to enumerate the major facts.

- In the second half of the paper explain what the process of conducting the research was like for you. Evaluate yourself as a researcher.

- End your paper by stating what this research has meant to you personally and what difference, if any, it has made (or will make) in your life. Give specific examples.

Think of this paper as being an introduction to a topic that most people don't know much about. Write like the authority you have now become.

Finally, now that you have some expertise in your field, share what you've learned with others through writing and speaking. You can:

- Write a letter to the editor of your local newspaper

- Offer to give an informal talk at your library

- Organize a discussion group for your topic

- Write an article and send it out for publication

- Call local businesses and organizations and offer your information and services

If you have completed an extended research project, you have learned what it means to know a subject well enough to speak and write about it with authority. Now that you've followed through one subject in a thorough way, you've gained the skills to do research on any subject, at any time, in any situation for the rest of your life.

The Appendix

Appendix A: Sample Student Papers

- A Paper Using the MLA Style of Documentation
- A Paper Using the Classic Footnote and Bibliography System
- A Paper Using Endnotes and Bibliography
- A Paper Using the APA Style

Appendix B: A List of Important Sources

- General Indexes and Other Listings of Books and Articles
- General References
- Specialized References
- Unusual Sources

A Paper Using the MLA Style of Documentation

The title
gives writer's
perspective—
not just the title
of the story.

A Parent's Reading of "Hansel and Gretel"

Donna Pesiri

Fairy tales, which seem to be aimed at children, often ad-

dress issues faced by both children and parents. In a way,

these stories teach lessons as important to the parents as they

are to the children.

The essay
begins with a
thesis sentence.

One of the most famous fairy tales, "Hansel and Gretel,"

is about how children part from their parents—how they gain

self-control and independence.

The essay is
built around
one primary
example of
the thesis.

Early in the story, Hansel and Gretel's parents disagree

about what action should be taken to ease their burden. The

stepmother wants to abandon the children in the forest; the fa-

ther feels the children should remain at home. Some critics inter-

Writer sets
up several
quotations.

pret this conflict in social terms. James M. Taggart writes about

Writer weaves
together several
secondary
sources.

the meaning of the story to poor people in Spain and Mexico

who know "food scarcity" from experience (444–45); Jack

Writer uses
brief quotations
rather than
chopping up
her paper.

Zipes also sees the story as "the struggle against poverty" (32).

Thinking as a parent, I saw this conflict as the ambivalence par-

ents feel about sending their children out into the world. Parents

realize they cannot shelter children forever. Children must learn

to take charge of their own lives. At the same time, parents fear for their children's safety and feel guilty over leaving "children alone in the forest" (Grimm 56).

Quotation from primary source.

The two parents in the story seem to represent two sides of real parents' feelings. According to Bruno Bettelheim, a child separates things into categories to help deal with difficult issues (66–67). In "Hansel and Gretel," he sees this separation not between an unsympathetic stepmother and a sympathetic father but between a good, dead mother, a bad stepmother, and an evil witch (162). Bettelheim's opinion differs slightly from mine but still shows that there is more than one side to a parent.

Writer paraphrases but still needs a citation.

The Grimms were concerned about the harshness of the parents in their original version. They revised the story, changing the mother to a stepmother and making the father weaker and sympathetic. According to John M. Ellis, their intention was not to upset children (72). I think the Grimms also understood that the process of growing up is difficult for parents as well as children. Complex issues are not easily resolved.

Citations include only page numbers because author's name is included in the text.

Hansel and Gretel overhear their parents' plan to abandon them. Gretel worries and cries. Hansel remains calm; he still has a naive trust that someone will always provide for them. As the children are led into the forest, Hansel leaves a trail of white stones behind him. These stones lead the children back home. The children are not ready to give up their secure existence.

Immaturity and inability to cope often send young people back to the safety of their parents' homes. As Bettelheim explains, regression is an initial reaction to the stresses of growing up (11).

The children are abandoned in the forest a second time, and their plans to return home fail. Hansel and Gretel discover that they cannot delay growing up any longer. The children meet a white bird that leads them to a candy house. The bird is the inevitable course of nature—it leads them to face reality and confront their situation. In fairy tales it is common for animals to serve as ''helpers'' and ''guides'' (Bettelheim 162).

Being suddenly thrust into a position of responsibility and having freedom of choice are hard for many young people to handle. The candy house is temptation. Without regard for consequences, Hansel and Gretel attack the house and eat uncontrollably. The children unleash a self-destructive force—the witch. The children must gain self-control or be destroyed. Max Luthi calls the witch ''the destructive power of the unconscious'' (64). Bettelheim calls the house ''tempting'' but sees it as a symbol of the ''good mother'' who offers food and comfort. The children's ''oral greediness'' is another attempt at regression (161).

Until this point, Gretel has been passive and dependent on her parents or on Hansel. Facing death at the hands of the

Writer credits
even quotations
of single words.

A Paper Using the MLA Style of Documentation 191

witch, Gretel breaks down and cries, "Please, God, help us."

The witch shouts back, "You can stop all that bawling, it'll do

you no good" (Grimm 61). This interchange forces Gretel to find

strength that she never thought she had. She uses her new-

found skills to defeat the witch and set Hansel free. I like this

part of the story the most because it shows that girls are able to

grow into intelligent, strong, and independent women. As Alison

Lurie says of fairy tales in general:

> These stories suggest a society in which women are
>
> as competent and active as men. . . . Gretel, not
>
> Hansel, defeats the witch. (42)

Bettelheim makes similar observations about the importance of

Gretel's transformation. After the examples of the evil step-

mother and the witch, it is "important to see that a female can

be a rescuer as well as a destroyer" (164). He cites the exam-

ple of a woman who has loved "Hansel and Gretel" since child-

hood. As an adult she realized why she loved the story so

much: it had helped her to settle an uneasy relationship with her

brother. She was very dependent on her older brother as they

were growing up and resented it (16–17).

The children find valuable treasure hidden in the witch's

house and gather it up. Hansel and Gretel have gained self-

Writer emphasizes her own original idea before bringing in the critics.

A strong lead-in to a quotation.

A good example of a longer quotation set off from the text and using ellipses.

control, self-esteem, knowledge, and independence. They have become enriched by experience. Hansel and Gretel find their way back home. The father welcomes back his successful children. Now the family is able to develop a mature relationship and live happily ever after. "Those who are exposed to danger can naturally perish in it; but they can also grow in it" (Luthi 66).

I agree with Bettelheim's view that adults should not interpret for children. Children will understand the stories on a subconscious level and will choose the parts that help them the most. It is just as important for the adult storyteller to know the meanings behind the tales. This knowledge, Bettelheim says, increases the benefits to the child "through a shared experience with another human being who, though an adult, can fully appreciate the feelings and reactions of the child" (155–56).

The story becomes an example of the writer's thesis.

When I was a child, I never analyzed fairy tales. I liked what I read, not giving much thought to why. Now I have a new appreciation for the stories when I read them to my children.

Works Cited

Bettelheim, Bruno. The Uses of Enchantment. New York: Knopf, 1976.

Ellis, John M. One Fairy Story Too Many: The Brothers Grimm and Their Tales.
Chicago: U of Chicago P, 1983.

Grimm, Jacob, and Wilhelm Grimm. Selected Tales. Ed. and trans. David Luke.
London: Penguin, 1982.

Lurie, Alison. "Fairy Tale Liberation." New York Review of Books 17 Dec. 1970:
42–44.

Luthi, Max. Once Upon a Time: On the Nature of Fairy Tales. New York: Ungar,
1970.

Taggart, James M. " 'Hansel and Gretel' in Spain and Mexico," Journal of
American Folklore 99 (Oct.–Dec. 1986): 435–60.

Zipes, Jack. Breaking the Magic Spell: Radical Theories of Folk and Fairy Tales.
Austin: U of Texas P, 1979.

A Paper Using the Classic Footnote and Bibliography System

A Parent's Reading of "Hansel and Gretel"

Donna Pesiri

Fairy tales, which seem to be aimed at children, often address issues faced by both children and parents. In a way, these stories teach lessons as important to the parents as they are to the children.

One of the most famous fairy tales, "Hansel and Gretel," is about how children part from their parents—how they gain self-control and independence.

Early in the story, Hansel and Gretel's parents disagree about what action should be taken to ease their burden. The stepmother wants to abandon the children in the forest; the father feels the children should remain at home. Some critics interpret this conflict in social terms. James M. Taggart writes about the meaning of the story to poor people in Spain and Mexico who know "food scarcity" from experience;[1] Jack Zipes also sees the story as "the struggle against poverty."[2] Thinking as an adult and parent, I saw this as the ambivalence parents feel about sending their children out into the world. Parents realize they cannot shelter children forever. Children must

---

[1] James M. Taggart, "'Hansel and Gretel' in Spain and Mexico," Journal of American Folklore 99 (Oct.–Dec. 1986), 444–45.
[2] Jack Zipes, Breaking the Magic Spell: Radical Theories of Folk and Fairy Tales (Austin: U of Texas P, 1979), 32.

learn to take charge of their own lives. At the same time, parents fear for their children's safety and feel guilty over leaving "children alone in the forest."[3]

The two parents in the story seem to represent two sides of real parents' feelings. According to Bruno Bettelheim, a child separates things into categories to help deal with difficult issues.[4] In "Hansel and Gretel," he sees this separation not between an unsympathetic stepmother and a sympathetic father but between a good, dead mother, a bad stepmother, and an evil witch.[5] Bettelheim's opinion differs slightly from mine but still shows that there is more than one side to a parent.

The Grimms were concerned about the harshness of the parents in their original version. They revised the story, changing the mother to a stepmother and making the father weaker and sympathetic. According to John M. Ellis, their intention was not to upset children.[6] I think the Grimms also understood that the process of growing up is difficult for parents as well as children. Complex issues are not easily resolved.

Hansel and Gretel overhear their parents' plan to abandon them. Gretel worries and cries. Hansel remains calm; he still has a naive trust that someone will always provide for them. As the children are led into the forest, Han-

---

[3] Jacob Grimm and Wilhelm Grimm, Selected Tales, Ed. and trans. David Luke (London: Penguin, 1982), 56.

[4] Bruno Bettelheim, The Uses of Enchantment (New York: Knopf, 1976), 66–67.

[5] Bettelheim 162.

[6] John M. Ellis, One Fairy Story Too Many: The Brothers Grimm and Their Tales (Chicago: U of Chicago P, 1983), 72.

196 The Appendix

sel leaves a trail of white stones behind him. These stones lead the children back home. The children are not ready to give up their secure existence. Immaturity and inability to cope often send young people back to the safety of their parents' homes. Bettelheim says that regression is an initial reaction to the stresses of growing up.[7]

The children are abandoned in the forest a second time, and their plans to return home fail. Hansel and Gretel discover that they cannot delay growing up any longer. The children meet a white bird that leads them to a candy house. The bird is the inevitable course of nature—it leads them to face reality and confront their situation. In fairy tales it is common for animals to serve as "helpers" and "guides."[8]

Being suddenly thrust into a position of responsibility and having freedom of choice are hard for many young people to handle. The candy house is temptation. Without regard for consequences, Hansel and Gretel attack the house and eat uncontrollably. The children unleash a self-destructive force— the witch. The children must gain self-control or be destroyed. Max Luthi calls the witch "the destructive power of the unconscious."[9] Bettelheim calls the house "tempting" but sees it as a symbol of the "good mother" who offers food and comfort. The children's "oral greediness" is another attempt at regression.[10]

---

[7] Bettelheim 11.

[8] Bettelheim 162.

[9] Max Luthi, Once Upon a Time: On the Nature of Fairy Tales (New York: Ungar, 1970), 64.

[10] Bettelheim 161.

Until this point, Gretel has been passive and dependent on her parents

or on Hansel. Facing death at the hands of the witch, Gretel breaks down

and cries, "Please, God, help us." The witch shouts back, "You can stop all

that bawling, it'll do you no good."[11] This interchange forces Gretel to find

strength that she never thought she had. She uses her new-found skills to

defeat the witch and set Hansel free. I like this part of the story the most be-

cause it shows that girls are able to grow into intelligent, strong, and inde-

pendent women. As Alison Lurie says of fairy tales in general:

> These stories suggest a society in which women are as compe-
>
> tent and active as men. . . . Gretel, not Hansel, defeats the
>
> witch.[12]

Bettelheim makes similar observations about the importance of Gretel's

transformation. After the examples of the evil stepmother and the witch, it is

"important to see that a female can be a rescuer as well as a destroyer."[13]

He cites the example of a woman who loved "Hansel and Gretel" since she

was a child. As an adult she realized why she loved the story so much: it

had helped her to settle an uneasy relationship with her brother. She

was very dependent on her older brother as they were growing up and

resented it.[14]

The children find valuable treasure hidden in the witch's house and

---

[11] Grimm 61.

[12] Alison Lurie, "Fairy Tale Liberation," New York Review of Books (17 Dec. 1970), 42.

[13] Bettelheim 164.

[14] Bettelheim 16–17.

gather it up. Hansel and Gretel have gained self-control, self-esteem, knowledge, and independence. They have become enriched by experience. Hansel and Gretel find their way back home. The father welcomes back his successful children. Now the family is able to develop a mature relationship and live happily ever after. "Those who are exposed to danger can naturally perish in it; but they can also grow in it."[15]

I agree with Bettelheim's view that adults should not interpret for children. Children will understand the stories on a subconscious level and will choose the parts that help them the most. It is just as important for the adult storyteller to know the meanings behind the tales. This knowledge increases the benefits to the child "through a shared experience with another human being who, though an adult, can fully appreciate the feelings and reactions of the child."[16]

When I was a child, I never analyzed fairy tales. I liked what I read, not giving much thought to why. Now I have a new appreciation for the stories when I read them to my children.

---

[15] Luthi 66.
[16] Bettelheim 155–56.

Bibliography

Bettelheim, Bruno. The Uses of Enchantment. New York: Knopf, 1976.

Ellis, John M. One Fairy Story Too Many: The Brothers Grimm and Their Tales.

   Chicago: U of Chicago P, 1983.

Grimm, Jacob, and Wilhelm Grimm. Selected Tales. Ed. and trans. David Luke.

   London: Penguin, 1982.

Lurie, Alison. "Fairy Tale Liberation." New York Review of Books (17 Dec. 1970):

   42–44.

Luthi, Max. Once Upon a Time: On the Nature of Fairy Tales. New York: Ungar,

   1970.

Taggart, James M. " 'Hansel and Gretel' in Spain and Mexico." Journal of

   American Folklore 99 (Oct.–Dec. 1986): 435–60.

Zipes, Jack. Breaking the Magic Spell: Radical Theories of Folk and Fairy Tales.

   Austin: U of Texas P, 1979.

A Paper Using Endnotes and Bibliography

A Parent's Reading of "Hansel and Gretel"

Donna Pesiri

Fairy tales, which seem to be aimed at children, often address issues faced by both children and parents. In a way, these stories teach lessons as important to the parents as they are to the children. One of the most famous fairy tales, "Hansel and Gretel," is about how children part from their parents—how they gain self-control and independence.

Early in the story, Hansel and Gretel's parents disagree about what action should be taken to ease their burden. The stepmother wants to abandon the children in the forest; the father feels the children should remain at home. Some critics interpret this conflict in social terms. James M. Taggart writes about the meaning of the story to poor people in Spain and Mexico who know "food scarcity" from experience;[1] Jack Zipes also sees the story as "the struggle against poverty."[2] Thinking as an adult and parent, I saw this as the ambivalence parents feel about sending their children out into the world. Parents realize they cannot shelter children forever. Children must learn to take charge of their own lives. At the same time, parents fear for their children's safety and feel guilty over leaving "children alone in the forest."[3]

The two parents in the story seem to represent two sides of real parents' feelings. According to Bruno Bettelheim, a child separates things into categories to help deal with difficult issues.[4] In "Hansel and Gretel," he sees this separation not between an unsympathetic stepmother and a sympathetic father but between a good, dead mother, a bad stepmother, and an evil witch.[5] Bettelheim's opinion differs slightly from mine but still shows that there is more than one side to a parent.

The Grimms were concerned about the harshness of the parents in their original version. They revised the story, changing the mother to a step-mother and making the father weaker and sympathetic. According to John M. Ellis, their intention was not to upset children.[6] I think the Grimms also understood that the process of growing up is difficult for parents as well as children. Complex issues are not easily resolved.

Hansel and Gretel overhear their parents' plan to abandon them. Gretel worries and cries. Hansel remains calm; he still has a naive trust that someone will always provide for them. As the children are led into the forest, Hansel leaves a trail of white stones behind him. These stones lead the children back home. The children are not ready to give up their secure existence. Immaturity and inability to cope often send young people back to the safety of their parents' homes. Bettelheim says that regression is an initial reaction to the stresses of growing up.[7]

The children are abandoned in the forest a second time, and their plans to return home fail. Hansel and Gretel discover that they cannot delay growing up any longer. The children meet a white bird that leads them to a candy house. The bird is the inevitable course of nature—it leads them to face reality and confront their situation. In fairy tales it is common for animals to serve as "helpers" and "guides."[8]

Being suddenly thrust into a position of responsibility and having freedom of choice are hard for many young people to handle. The candy house is temptation. Without regard for consequences, Hansel and Gretel attack the house and eat uncontrollably. The children unleash a self-destructive force— the witch. The children must gain self-control or be destroyed. Max Luthi calls the witch "the destructive power of the unconscious."[9] Bettelheim calls the house "tempting" but sees it as a symbol of the "good mother" who offers food and comfort. The children's "oral greediness" is another attempt at regression.[10]

Until this point, Gretel has been passive and dependent on her parents or on Hansel. Facing death at the hands of the witch, Gretel breaks down and cries, "Please, God, help us." The witch shouts back, "You can stop all that bawling, it'll do you no good."[11] This interchange forces Gretel to find strength that she never thought she had. She uses her new-found skills to defeat the witch and set Hansel free. I like this part of the story the most because it shows that girls are able to grow into intelligent, strong, and independent women. As Alison Lurie says of fairy tales in general:

These stories suggest a society in which women are as competent and active as men. . . . Gretel, not Hansel, defeats the witch.[12]

Bettelheim makes similar observations about the importance of Gretel's transformation. After the examples of the evil stepmother and the witch it is "important to see that a female can be a rescuer as well as a destroyer."[13] He cites the example of a woman who loved "Hansel and Gretel" since she was a child. As an adult she realized why she loved the story so much: it had helped her to settle an uneasy relationship with her brother. She was very dependent on her older brother as they were growing up and resented it.[14]

The children find valuable treasure hidden in the witch's house and gather it up. Hansel and Gretel have gained self-control, self-esteem, knowledge, and independence. They have become enriched by experience. Hansel and Gretel find their way back home. The father welcomes back his successful children. Now the family is able to develop a mature relationship and live happily ever after. "Those who are exposed to danger can naturally perish in it; but they can also grow in it."[15]

I agree with Bettelheim's view that adults should not interpret for children. Children will understand the stories on a subconscious level and will choose the parts that help them the most. It is just as important for the adult storyteller to know the meanings behind the tales. This knowledge increases the benefits to the child "through a shared experience with another human being who, though an adult, can fully appreciate the feelings and reactions of the child."[16]

When I was a child, I never analyzed fairy tales. I liked what I read, not giving much thought to why. Now I have a new appreciation for the stories when I read them to my children.

Notes

Pesiri

[1] James M. Taggart, " 'Hansel and Gretel' in Spain and Mexico," Journal of American Folklore 99 (Oct.–Dec. 1986), 444–45.

[2] Jack Zipes, Breaking the Magic Spell: Radical Theories of Folly and Fairy Tales (Austin: U of Texas P, 1979), 32.

[3] Jacob Grimm and Wilhelm Grimm, Selected Tales, Ed. and trans. David Luke (London: Penguin, 1982), 56.

[4] Bruno Bettelheim, The Uses of Enchantment (New York: Knopf, 1976), 66–67.

[5] Bettelheim 162.

[6] John M. Ellis, One Fairy Story Too Many: The Brothers Grimm and Their Tales (Chicago: U of Chicago P, 1983), 72.

[7] Bettelheim 11.

[8] Bettelheim 162.

[9] Max Luthi, Once Upon a Time: On the Nature of Fairy Tales (New York: Ungar, 1970), 64.

[10] Bettelheim 161.

[11] Grimm 61.

[12] Alison Lurie, "Fairy Tale Liberation," New York Review of Books (17 Dec. 1970), 42.

[13] Bettelheim 164.

[14] Bettelheim 16–17.

[15] Luthi 66.

[16] Bettelheim 155–56.

Bibliography

Pesiri

Bettelheim, Bruno. The Uses of Enchantment. New York: Knopf, 1976.

Ellis, John M. One Fairy Story Too Many: The Brothers Grimm and Their Tales.
Chicago: U of Chicago P, 1983.

Grimm, Jacob, and Wilhelm Grimm. Selected Tales. Ed. and trans. David Luke.
London: Penguin, 1982.

Lurie, Alison. "Fairy Tale Liberation." New York Review of Books (17 Dec. 1970):
42–44.

Luthi, Max. Once Upon a Time: On the Nature of Fairy Tales. New York: Ungar,
1970.

Taggart, James M. " 'Hansel and Gretel' in Spain and Mexico." Journal of
American Folklore 99 (Oct.–Dec. 1986): 435–60.

Zipes, Jack. Breaking the Magic Spell: Radical Theories of Folk and Fairy Tales.
Austin: U of Texas P, 1979.

Sleeping Pills: Help or Hindrance?
Steven Pangiotidis
Sociology 131 HD
Professor Ferris
Term Report
4/23/91

ABSTRACT:

Sleeping pills are harmful drugs that are often taken for sleep deprivation. They have become a real epidemic, and the statistics to prove it are amazing. Over-prescribing is the main cause of the problem. Doctors are prescribing unneeded medications, but that's not the only reason for the crisis. Many people with sleep disorders are abusing these drugs and can't overcome their addictions. They take the drugs because they feel a psychological need as well as to sleep better. But the effects of sleeping pills are very harmful. They reduce the activity of the brain and nervous system, and can cause both mental and physical addiction. An over-dose can cause coma or death. Besides being ineffective in curing the sleep disorder, they can often make the problem worse. Until doctors stop overprescribing and many of the products are taken off the store shelves, the epidemic will increase. In the future, if we can get all our facts straight on sleeping pills, we can turn the epidemic around.

Thesis: Sleeping pills—widely overprescribed—are not the answer to sleep deprivation because they do little to help the situation, and their side effects, which include addiction, can be very harmful.

Topic Outline

I. Introduction

    A. Choice of many

    B. Definition

II. Long-term sleeping pill epidemic

    A. Government statistics

    B. Overprescribing

    C. Statistics from pharmaceutical fact file

III. Discussion of Problem

    A. Addiction

    B. Other Dangers

    C. Ineffectiveness

IV. Solutions

    A. Stopping overprescribing

    B. Taking products off supermarket shelves

    C. Eliminating the abuse

        1. Overcoming addiction

        2. Poem about need for sleeping pills

V. Conclusion

    A. Publishing facts

    B. Turnaround of epidemic

People who suffer from sleep deprivation try many different options to go to sleep. Some exercise, others eat, and some even count sheep. However, many take the low road and go with sleeping pills.

Sleeping pills are drugs used to calm people down or make them sleep. They are usually barbiturates and vary in their strength and duration of effects. They reduce the activity of the brain and the rest of the nervous system. However, sleeping pills—widely overprescribed—are not the answer to sleep deprivation because they do little to help the situation, and their side effects, which include addiction, can be very harmful. An overdose can cause coma—or even death.

Thesis statement.

The sleeping pill epidemic has existed for some time now, but only recently have we finally begun to realize it. In the United States alone, in 1964, the first year such data were collected, "over 32 million prescriptions for sleeping pills were written" (Trubo 1978, p. 74). By now, the numbers must be staggering. The problem is largely due to the fact that these drugs are being overprescribed, or at least not properly prescribed. According to government statistics, for example, about 30 percent of sleeping pill prescriptions are given to people whose problem

After a quotation, APA style cites author, date, and page.

is "primarily psychological in origin"; another 25 percent go to those with medical conditions that won't respond to sleeping pills, while still another 18 percent go to patients "with ill-defined or vague symptoms that usually don't require drug treatment" (Hales 1981, pp. 281–82). As long ago as 1973, Dr. Ernest L. Hartmann found that "As many as four out of five sleep pill prescriptions are inappropriate or ineffective" (p. 41).

Author and date have been given, so only the page is cited.

This paragraph is a good example of an assertion backed by evidence—interweaving several sources.

A few of the mind-boggling statistics concerning sleeping pills have been compiled by Donald R. Sweeney (1989):

- Sleeping medications are "the most widely used class of drugs" in this country.

- Doctors write "between 20 and 30 million prescriptions a year" for sleeping pills and tranquilizers.

- Americans spend "over $200 million a year" for sleeping medications.

- "Over 4 percent of the population—nearly 11 million" people—use prescription sleep medicines.

- An "even larger group" uses over-the-counter relaxants.

- "About half of all patients in hospitals" are given sedatives—at least once.

- In the U.S. alone, we consume "approximately 600 tons of sleep medications" (p. 232).

Here's the kicker: In many cases these pills don't work, make the problem worse, or result in serious side effects. Further, Dionne Hales (1981) reports that the Department of Health and Human Services lists sleeping pills as the cause of about a third of the drug-related deaths each year.

Some people take large amounts of sleeping pills to escape tension, as well as to sleep better, which has a lot to do with the alarming statistics. Such doses produce intoxication similar to that caused by alcohol. Users' speech becomes slurred, and their coordination and judgment become poor. People who regularly take large doses of sleeping pills develop an addiction. "When addicted people try to stop using the pills," said Hartmann (1973), "they suffer convulsions, body twitchings, and severe nervousness" (p. 43). Even worse, he also pointed out that sudden withdrawal from the drugs can cause death. Addicts can end their dependence on sleeping pills only by gradually reducing the amount they take.

In APA style, cite the date after the author's name.

The dangers of sleeping pills listed by Hales (1981) should convince anyone to stop taking them:

- Fatal overdoses, particularly if combined with alcohol or any medications affecting the nervous system

- Harmful effects on people who have chronic medical problems—particularly on those with diseases of the kidneys, liver, or lungs

- "Hangover" effects that impair daytime coordination, driving skills, logical thinking, and mood

- Confusion, hallucinations, and other adverse effects in the elderly

- If taken in pregnancy, possible birth defects for the child

- Difficulty in awakening to respond to a fire alarm, crying child, or other crisis (p. 134)

The irony is that with all these risks, sleeping pills don't work. Hale (1981) described "exacerbation of the initial sleep problem" and "disruption of normal sleep stages" (p. 134). Treating a sleep disorder with these drugs may produce sleep for a few days, or even a few weeks, but in the long run they are just making the problem worse. When I interviewed Dr. Michael J. Thorpy (1990), he said, "As a lasting solution to a sleep problem, sleeping pills do little, if any, good. And they can do considerable harm." I think that Dr. Nathaniel Kleitman (1990), a sleep therapist, put it best when he said that "in a sense sleeping pills are like throat lozenges, which soothe the irritation but do not cure the cough" (qtd. in Toufexis, p. 79).

The writer has a clear point of view and marshalls strong quotations in its defense.

Note the use of "qtd. in" [quoted in].

What are the solutions to this epidemic? One way to avoid the dangers of sleeping pills is to end the senseless prescribing. Doctors should stop misusing their authority, and when a patient asks for medication, they shouldn't be so quick to pick up their pens. First they should examine the patient and see if he or she really needs the drugs. Then, and only then, should they even consider writing out the slip.

A New York Times article (1988) reported that in the United States, these powerful drugs can be obtained only with a prescription ("Exploring," p. 26). I disagree because I think that many of these drugs are still out there in the supermarket aisles where depressed teenagers, or anyone for that matter, can have easy access to them. I also think that many of these dangerous drugs are still sitting out on store shelves disguised as cold remedies and other medications—for example, NyQuil, "the nighttime sniffling, sneezing, coughing, aching, stuffy head, fever, so you can [go into a coma]" medicine. Once I took some NyQuil, which contains an antihistamine, for a cold and it put me into such a deep, long sleep, that when I woke up (which seemed like weeks later), I didn't remember anything.

One thing I can do, as well as other people with sleep problems, is to stay away from sleeping pills. In my interview with Dr.

Thorpy (1990), he said that "the only people who can change this problem are the ones who are having trouble sleeping." There should be more doctors like Dr. Thorpy, who always discourages his patients from taking any sleeping pills.

But people just can't overcome their addiction to these pills, even when they know perfectly well that "they rarely work and never induce 'normal' sleep" (Dement 1972, p. 130). The following poem, written by Ryah Goodman (1980), reveals the deep psychological needs that make a person turn to sleeping pills:

> The light within me clicks,
>
> Who put out the light?
>
> It is dark.
>
> I am alone, afraid.
>
> Mother, Mother,
>
> I can't sleep.
>
> My mother does not come.
>
> My mother is dead.
>
> One pill,
>
> Two pills,
>
> Three pills,
>
> Mother me, pills. (qtd. in Hales p. 130)

In conclusion, I don't think that sleeping pills are the answer to our sleep problems. They rarely help; in fact, they usually make the matter worse. Dr. Thorpy (1990) said, "As a rule, I am not enthusiastic about the use of these products in sleep depriva-tion. Besides being ineffective, especially in long-term use, they can cause nausea, vomiting, and other side effects." I can only hope that I'm not the only one to learn these facts and have a better perspective on this topic. Perhaps in the future we can learn to make the right decisions when coming across sleeping pills. We all have to get the necessary facts in order to do our part in turning this crisis around and stopping the senseless abuse of these very dangerous drugs.

References

Dement, W. C. (1972). Some must watch, while some must sleep. San Francisco: Stanford Alumni Association.

Note the APA format for references.

Exploring the forces of sleep. (1988, April 17). New York Times, p. D 26.

Hales, D. (1981). The complete book of sleep. Boston: Addison-Wesley.

Hartmann, E. L. (1973). The function of sleep. New Haven: Yale University Press.

Sweeney, D. R. (1989). Overcoming insomnia. G. P. Putnam's Sons.

Thorpy, M. J. (1990, March 27). (Sleep Therapist, Montefiore Hospital) Telephone Interview.

Note the variety of sources—including books, articles, and an interview.

Toufexis, A. (1990, December 17). Drowsy America. Time, pp. 78–81.

Trubo, R. (1978). How to get a good night's sleep. Boston: Little, Brown.

A List of Important Sources

The following list includes the most basic resources. Your librarian or teacher may suggest more specific references. You'll find these reference materials in one or more of the following formats: *print, film,* or *electronic*. Whenever possible, begin your search with the computer because it is comprehensive and takes less time to use.

I. General Indexes and Other Listings of Books and Articles

American Statistical Index. A monthly index of all U.S. government statistical publications.

Applied Science and Technology Index. A quarterly index to articles on subjects in electronics, engineering, fabric technology, food production, and fossil energy.

Bibliographic Index: A Cumulative Bibliography of Bibliographies. Lists, by subject, bibliographies published both separately and in books and periodicals.

Biography Index: A Cumulative Index to Biographical Material in Books and Magazines. A comprehensive, international listing of biographical information, including major historical figures. Indexed by name and by profession.

Book Review Digest. Gives excerpts of selected reviews of fiction and non-fiction books in all fields.

Books in Print. Use this guide to locate books in print by title, author, or subject. See also *Paperback Books in Print*.

Citation Indexes: *Arts and Humanities Citation Index*
Science Citation Index
Social Sciences Citation Index

Each volume has four parts: (1) "Permuterm Index"—lists specific authors covered; (2) "Citation Index"—lists where a particular author was cited by other authors that year; (3) "Source Index"—lists what articles an author published that year; (4) "Corporate Index"—lists articles published in specific geographical regions.

Cumulative Book Index. International bibliography of books published in English worldwide.

Essay and General Literature Index . A guide to individual essays or chapters in books on topics not normally listed in standard indexes or library catalogs.

General Science Index. Indexes articles from over 100 science periodicals.

Guide to U.S. Government Publications. Two-part guide; issued annually.

Humanities Index. Indexes articles from nearly 300 periodicals in the arts, classics, languages, literature, philosophy, and religion. Updated quarterly.

Magazine Index Plus. Indexes over 400 popular and general-interest periodicals. Monthly.

National Newspaper Index. Indexes articles from five major newspapers: *Christian Science Monitor, Los Angeles Times, New York Times, Wall Street Journal*, and *The Washington Post*. Monthly.

New York Times Index: A Book of Record. Indexes topics covered by *The New York Times*, annually since 1851.

Readers' Guide to Periodical Literature. Indexes articles, by author and subject, from 200 general magazines.

Sheehy, Eugene P. *Guide to Reference Books*. Lists all reference books published in the United States.

Social Sciences Index. Indexes articles in anthropology, economics, law, political science, psychology, and sociology. Updated quarterly.

Vertical File Index. New York: Wilson, 1935–. Indexes, by title and subject, pamphlets on all subjects.

II. General References

Atlases

Hammond Atlas of the World. Maplewood, NJ: Hammond, 1993. Includes 160 pages of maps, over 115,000 entries in index.

The New York Times Atlas of the World. Third Revised Concise Edition. New York: Times Books, 1992. Includes 146 pages of maps, over 100,000 entries in index.

Biographies

Annual Obituary. Obituaries of prominent individuals who have died during the year.

Current Biography. Gives biographical data about people currently making the news. 1940–.

Dictionary of American Biography. Contains lengthy articles on Americans who are no longer living.

Dictionary of National Biography. Contains lengthy articles on British people who are no longer living.

McGraw-Hill Encyclopedia of World Biography. Illustrated, with short biographies of world figures.

New York Times Obituary Index. Covers national and international figures; indexed by the year of death.

Who's Who in America. Chicago: Marquis, 1899–present. Provides current information about prominent people who are still living. (See also other *Who's Who* and *Who Was Who* guides.)

Directories

Encyclopedia of Associations. Lists, with addresses, professional associations.

Foundation Directory. Lists, with addresses, philanthropic foundations and foundations for specialized studies.

Dictionaries

American Heritage Dictionary. Contains excellent photographs and illustrations.

Oxford English Dictionary (OED). 13 vols. Gives the full historical development of English words.

Webster's New Universal Unabridged Dictionary of the English Language.
The dictionary most often cited.

Encyclopedias

Collier's Encyclopedia. Good general information source for contemporary
subjects.

Encyclopedia Americana. Good for scientific and technical topics.

Encyclopaedia Britannica. The most definitive, comprehensive encyclopedia. Annual supplement, *Britannica Book of the Year.*

McGraw-Hill Encyclopedia of Science and Technology. Articles on all areas
of science and technology. Updated annually (*McGraw-Hill Yearbook of
Science and Technology*).

Yearbooks and Almanacs

Facts on File. Weekly summaries of U.S. and world news.

The World Almanac and Book of Facts. An excellent source for statistics in
many fields.

III. Specialized References

Anthropology, see Sociology and Anthropology

Art

Art Index

Encyclopedia of World Art. 15 vols. with supplements.

Oxford Companion to Art. (See also Oxford Companion to Twentieth Century Art.)

Astronomy, see Ecology and Earth Sciences

Biology

Biological and Agricultural Index

Encyclopedia of the Biological Sciences

Informational Sources in the Life Sciences

Magill's Survey of Science: Life Science Series. 6 vols.

Black Studies, see Ethnic Studies

Business and Economics

Business Index

Business Information Sources

Business Periodicals Index

Consumers Index

Encyclopedia of Business Information Sources

Information Sources in Economics

McGraw-Hill Dictionary of Modern Economics

Wall Street Journal Index

Chemistry

Chemistry Abstracts

Condensed Chemical Dictionary

CRC Handbook of Chemistry and Physics

Encyclopedia of Chemistry

Kirk-Othmer Encyclopedia of Chemical Technology

Communications (Journalism and Media)

Cates, S. A. *Journalism: A Guide to the Reference Literature*

Communications Abstracts

Encyclopedia of American Journalism

International Encyclopedia of Communications

Speech Index

Computer Science

Computer Abstracts

Computer Literature Index

Criminal Justice, see Law and Criminal Justice

Dance, see Music and Dance

Drama, see Theatre

Ecology and Earth Sciences

Encyclopedia of Earth Sciences

Encyclopedia of Environmental Science

Encyclopedia of Field and General Geology

Environmental Abstracts

Grzimel's Encyclopedia of Ecology

McGraw-Hill Encyclopedia of Environmental Science

World Resources

Economics, see Business and Economics

Education

Child Development Abstracts and Bibliography

Current Index to Journals in Education

Education Index

ERIC Resources in Education

Engineering

Engineering Index Monthly and Author Index

McGraw-Hill Dictionary of Engineering

English, see Language and Literature

Environment, see Ecology and Earth Sciences

Ethnic Studies

Dictionary of American Immigration History

Harvard Encyclopedia of American Ethnic Groups

Index to Black Periodicals

Miller, Wayne, et al. *A Comprehensive Bibliography for the Study of American Minority Groups*

Minority Organizations: A National Directory

Film

Film Review Annual

Halliwell's Film and Video Guide

International Encyclopedia of Film

New York Times Film Review Index

Oxford Companion to Film

Folklore, see Religion and Mythology

Geology, see Ecology and Earth Sciences

Government, see Political Science

Health Care and Medicine

Cumulative Index to Nursing and Allied Health Literature

Dorland's Illustrated Medical Dictionary

Index Medicus

Introduction to Reference Sources in Health Sciences

Physicians' Desk Reference

History

Cambridge History Series. Ancient (12 vols.); *Latin America; Medieval;* (8 vols.); *Modern* (14 vols.)

Dictionary of American History

Historical Abstracts

Library Research Guide to History

Journalism, see Communications (Journalism and Media)

Language and Literature

Essay and General Literature Index

Granger's Index to Poetry

Holman, C. Hugh and William Harmon. *Handbook to Literature*

Language and Language Behavior Abstracts

Literary Criticism Index

MLA (Modern Language Association) International Bibliography

Modern Critical Interpretations Series, ed. Harold Bloom (over 150 vols.)

Oxford Companion to Literature. Separate volumes for American, Canadian, classical, English, French, Spanish, and German.

Penguin Companion to Literature. Separate volumes for American, English, European, classical, Oriental, and African.

Play Index

Short Story Index

Spiller, Robert, et al. *Literary History of the United States.*

Twayne Series. Separate volumes on specific authors and works.

Twentieth Century Views. Separate volumes on specific authors and works.

Law and Criminal Justice

Black's Law Dictionary

Criminal Justice Abstracts

Criminal Justice Periodicals Index
Encyclopedia of Crime and Justice
Encyclopedic Dictionary of International Law
Guide to American Law
Index to Legal Periodicals

Mathematics

Encyclopedic Dictionary of Mathematics
Prentice-Hall Encyclopedia of Math

Media, see Communications (Journalism and Media); also see Film

Medicine, see Health Care and Medicine

Music and Dance

Concise Oxford Dictionary of Ballet
Encyclopedia of Dance and Ballet
Encyclopedia of Folk, Country and Western Music
Music Index
New Grove Dictionary of Music and Musicians (20 vols.)
New Oxford Companion to Music
Performing Arts Research: A Guide to Information Sources
Popular Music: An Annotated Index of American Popular Songs

Mythology, see Religion and Mythology

Nursing, see Health Care and Medicine

Philosophy

Dictionary of Philosophy
Encyclopedia of Philosophy
Philosophers' Index
Research Guide to Philosophy

Physics

Current Physics Index

McGraw-Hill Encyclopedia of Physics

Physics Abstracts

Political Science

ABC Pol Sci: Advanced Bibliography of Contents, Political Science and
  Government

Congressional Quarterly

Information Sources of Political Science

International Political Science Abstracts

PAIS (Public Affairs Information Service Bulletin)

Statesmen's Yearbook

Vital Speeches

Psychology

Annual Review of Psychology

Encyclopedia of Psychology

Psychological Abstracts

Reed, Jeffrey, and Pam Baxter. Library Use: A Handbook for Psychology

Religion and Mythology

Encyclopedia of Religion

Index to Book Reviews in Religion

New Larousse Encyclopedia of Mythology

Readers Guide to the Great Religions

Religion and Theological Abstracts

See also Atlases and Concordances of the Bible.

Sociology and Anthropology

Abstracts in Anthropology

Encyclopedia of Sociology

Human Resources Abstracts

Social Work Research and Abstracts

Sociological Abstracts

Sociological Index

Sociology, A Guide to Reference and Information Sources

Theatre

Dramatic Criticism Index

McGraw-Hill Encyclopedia of World Drama

New York Times Theatre Reviews

Performing Arts Research: A Guide to Information Sources

Play Index

Women's Studies

Searing, S. *Introduction to Library Research in Women's Studies*

Statistical Handbook on Women in America

Women's Studies Abstracts

Women's Studies Encyclopedia

IV. Unusual Sources

The sources in this list do not fit easily into any category, but many of them can provide a good quotation, an anecdote, or an unusual fact to spark up your paper.

Adams, Cecil. *The Straight Dope*. New York: Ballantine, 1984.

———. *More Straight Dope*. New York: Ballantine, 1988. Provides answers to odd questions, such as how many square inches of skin are on the average human body.

Anatomy models. These are useful for medical topics and studies in anatomy; most college libraries have them.

Bartlett's Familiar Quotations. Sixteenth Edition. Boston: Little, Brown, 1992.

Baseball Encyclopedia: The Complete and Official Record of Major League Baseball. 9th ed. New York: Macmillan, 1990.

Benet, William Rose. *The Reader's Encyclopedia*. An encyclopedia of world literature.

Bragonia, Reginald, Jr., and David Fisher. *What's What: A Visual Glossary*. New York: Ballantine, 1981. Illustrates and names the parts of common objects.

Brewer's Dictionary of Phrase and Fable. New York: HarperCollins, 1989.

Bureau of Census Reports. Various reports, filled with all sorts of facts about American life. Based on census data collected every ten years.

Burnam, Tom. *The Dictionary of Misinformation: The Book to Set the Record Straight*. New York: HarperCollins, 1986.

Byrne, Josefa Heifetz. *Mrs. Byrne's Dictionary of Unusual, Obscure and Preposterous Words*. Secaucus, NJ: Citadel, 1974.

Chapman, Robert L., ed. *American Slang*. New York: HarperCollins, 1987.

Ciardi, John. *A Browser's Dictionary: A Compendium of Curious Expressions and Intriguing Facts*. New York: Harper & Row, 1980.

DeGregorio, William H. *The Complete Book of U.S. Presidents*. New York: Dembner, 1984.

Feldman, David. *Imponderables: The Solution to the Mysteries of Everyday Life*. New York: Wm. Morrow & Co., 1987. First of a series, organized by questions and answers, but with index. See also *Do Penguins Have Knees? Why Do Dogs Have Wet Noses?* and *Why Do Clocks Run Clockwise?*

Gloag, J. E. *A Short Dictionary of Furniture*. New York: Overlook Press, 1991.

Guinness's Book of World Records. New York: Bantam (Updated each year)

Heymann, Thomas. *On An Average Day*. . . . New York: Ballantine, 1989. Lists statistics on American life and habits.

Information Please! Almanac: The New Universe of Information. New York: Houghton. Published annually.

Jones, Judy and William Wilson. *An Incomplete Education*. New York: Ballantine, 1987. Provides a variety of information not easily found, such as explanations of the job titles in film production credits.

Kane, Joseph Nathan. *Famous First Facts*. New York: Wilson, 1981. Lists the first time for major events.

Katz, Bill, and Linda Katz. *Self Help: Fourteen Hundred Best Books on Personal Growth*. New York: Bowker, 1985.

Lapham, Lewis, Michael Pollan and Eric Etheridge. *Harper's Index Book*. New York: Holt, 1987. See also individual issues of *Harper's* magazine since 1986. Provides statistics with social and political implications—such as the number of millionaires on different presidents' cabinets.

Metcalf, Fred. *The Penguin Dictionary of Modern Humorous Quotations*. New York: Penguin, 1986.

Oxford Dictionary of Quotations. New York: Oxford, 1979.

Panatti, Charles. *Extraordinary Origins of Everyday Things*. New York: Harper, 1987. Inventions of common objects.

Peter, Laurence J. *Peter's Quotations: Ideas for Our Time*. New York: Bantam, 1983.

Wallechinsky, David, Irving Wallace, and Amy Wallace. *The Book of Lists*. New York, 1977. (See other books of lists in this series.)

Wiener, Philip P., ed. *Dictionary of the History of Ideas*. New York: Scribner's. (Several volumes)

Index